D1488557

UNLOCK!

7 Steps to Transform
your **Career** and
Realize your
Leadership Potential

Abhijeet Khadilkar

Copyright © 2020 by Abhijeet Khadilkar

All rights reserved.

Proudly printed in the United States by Vicara Books.

VICARA BOOKS | www.vicarabooks.com

All trademarks are the property of their respective companies.

Cover Design by Enosh Wilson

Inside Page Design by Verbinden Communication Pvt. Ltd., Bangalore, India

First Printing: July 2020

Cataloging-in-Publication Data is on file with the Library of Congress.

ISBN: 978-1-64687-030-1

Price: USD 24.95

Proudly Printed in the USA

Special Sales

Vicara Books are available at a special discount for bulk purchases for sales promotions and premiums, educational institutions or for use in corporate training programs. Special editions, including personalized covers, custom forewords and bonus content are also available.

For more information, email info@ideapresspublishing.com

ADVANCE PRAISE FOR *UNLOCK!*

"Stuck? *Unlock!* offers practical advice to professionals who need to jumpstart their careers. If you believe that your career growth is your #1 job, do yourself a favor and pick up this book. The frameworks and recommendations provided in *Unlock!* equip you to move quickly from frustration to action, while Khadilkar's to-the-point style makes this a compelling, as well as immensely useful read."

Jonathan Copulsky
former CMO, Deloitte Consulting, and faculty member,
Northwestern University

"It has been a joy to watch Abhijeet over the years as he raised the bar for himself while raising the bar for everyone else he touched. Abhijeet has a unique ability to help others discover their unique abilities. With that, he has helped people shape their careers for the better. *Unlock!* is where he has packaged his wisdom to bring this positive change at scale. Get a copy to change your life and get one more to change the life of someone you care."

Rajesh Setty
Co-Founder of Audvisor,
author of 'Six Foot World' and 15 other books

"Abhijeet is an absolute treasure. One of my favorite things about this book is that he writes openly about the importance of mindset, which in my opinion, is one of the top two indicators of success (along with emotional intelligence)."

Johanna Lyman

CEO of Next Gen Orgs and President of Bay Area Chapter of Conscious Capitalism

"When Abhijeet gives you advice, you listen. I do. Abhijeet is one of the most focused, committed, result-oriented yet helpful professionals I have come across. Supplement his passion for excellence with his knowledge and experience, and you get an unbeatable package – a concoction which invigorates you and forces you to think. I have had the privilege of working with Abhijeet directly on consulting assignments for global technology firms and to listen to his perspectives on work and on life. He is lively and authentic, and his guidance is pragmatic and applied readily to professional settings. I have had the privilege of reading parts of this book, and it has a clear stamp of Abhijeet's charm and wit. Must read!"

Aashish Chandorkar

Leading Management Consultant, columnist, and bestselling author of 'The Fadnavis Years'

"Managing your career is your most important job. But oftentimes it is hard to get started in our personal transformation journeys; too many questions and too much uncertainty cloud our vision. There are lots of armchair experts who dispense career advice, but moving from talk to action is difficult. I had the pleasure of working with Khadilkar early in his career, and over time witnessed his own transformation into a tech leader and (reluctant) career coach. In *Unlock!* he synthesizes a very practical, seven-step approach to define your personal strategy from his experience and shows you how to execute it to become the leader you are meant to be."

Alejandro Danylyszyn
Principal, Deloitte Consulting

"Abhijeet has continued to strive for doing not only what's best for business but also honing his leadership skills to bring out the best in his team."

Joe Pinto
Chief Customer Experience Officer, Pure Storage

"It is a common misconception in many graduate business programs that management and leadership are synonyms. Oftentimes, the tools and methodologies are oriented strictly toward the mechanics of management such as planning, organizing, staffing, directing, and controlling. As the workplace and the workforce evolve to ever more decentralized, remote, and autonomous architectures, good management hygiene will no longer suffice. It has to be combined with the core of good leadership – learning from failure, driving a culture of lessons learned, creating an environment of rapidly forming adaptive teams united by a common purpose, and, most importantly, building trust. *Unlock!* provides a real-world approach to developing strategies to unlock team potential through the practical application of leadership principles. Trust Abhijeet to provide an innovative framework that helps you figure out: where you want to go in your career, develop leadership skills, and build a personal brand, critical things you need to be successful in the

2020+ world. Investing in yourself always pays off, *Unlock!* is your career investment tool."

Tom Berghoff
Senior Vice President, Customer Experience at Cisco

"A practical handbook of tools, advice, and a step by step action plan, that will help you unleash the leader within you and skyrocket your career potential. It will put you on the path to have a more happy, fulfilled, and balanced life. During the past two decades, I have pleasantly observed Abhijeet growing from a young software quality engineer to a successful management consultant in digital transformation, a successful entrepreneur, and now an author. Abhijeet has always walked the talk, and in *Unlock!* he takes his life and career lessons into an easy to read, usable and valuable resource as a way of giving back to the community, especially in these disruptive times."

Danis Yadegar
Serial Entrepreneur, Angel Investor,
Managing Partner at WeMax Innovation Capital and former CEO, Arsin Corp

"With Unlock!, Abhijeet has codified all those soft dimensions, relationships, decisions, and attributes that go into the development of a healthy and robust professional career. He does so with relevant examples from contemporary business situations. An invaluable read for anyone looking to get more out of their career, regardless of what stage they may be at."

Kaushik Bhaumik
PhD, Angel investor, former EVP at Cognizant Technology Solutions
and Management Consultant

FOREWORD

How do you write a career guide for a world of work that feels as unstable and dangerous as walking across a field of lava?

Every part of our work environment is melting down. How we work. Where we work. What work we as humans do, as opposed to the artificial intelligence taking over many aspects of our jobs. We have seen entire industries disintegrate due to unexpected economic downturns and global health pandemics.

Can you still create a viable, meaningful and growing career under such conditions?

You can hack your way to financial or career success in one job or business, but to ensure long-term career health and stability, you need a systematic approach to career leadership. One that teaches a particular set of skills that allows you to continually identify shifts in your business environment and adjust your approach so that you consistently deliver results, regardless of external circumstances. In addition to these technical skills, you need to develop a true model of leadership that is humane, relational and focused on the long-term.

Abhijeet Khadilkar delivers this specific framework in this modern handbook for career leadership, *Unlock!*

I've personally known Abhijeet since 2009 when he was starting CareerTiger as a pro-bono service to coach people affected by the financial crisis.

I still remember our very first meeting.

It happened in June of 2009. We were scheduled to meet at the San Jose airport. My first book, *Escape from Cubicle Nation*, had recently launched. And I was right in the middle of a major book tour. I landed in San Jose and as a creature of habit stopped by the airport bookstore. As I was scrolling magazines and newspapers, something caught my eye in the newspaper section: Abhijeet on the cover of Silicon Valley's leading newspaper, the San Jose Mercury News! It was so serendipitous to meet him on the very day his expertise was recognized by his larger community.

Over the years, Abhijeet has demonstrated by personal example how to be a great leader in the corporate world. Not only has he developed domain expertise in tech, but he has always been generous to give back to the community in terms of career advice and mentoring.

I have a strange superpower of quickly identifying people who are both building significant bodies of work designed to transform the world for the better, and who do so in a way that engenders trust, optimism and confidence in their communities.

I am so glad that Abhijeet took the time to simplify complex topics, and then codify them in a way that you can apply to your work daily, in the form of useful tools and frameworks.

You are learning from a technical mentor who is also a person you can trust. That is a rare and valuable thing.

Every time I come across a business book, one of the questions I always have is: is this book based on a cool-sounding but never implemented idea, or one that has been road-tested in the real world with real people like you and me, delivering real results?

Unlock! is the real deal. Keep it on your desk as a reference. Share it with people in your network that you love and admire. Especially share it with your team at work.

The viability of our economy requires that we reengineer the way we prepare our workforce to adapt to change. The viability and meaning of our own, very personal bodies of work, will be determined by choosing to take leadership of our careers and our lives.

Unlock your leadership and you will help us all. We are counting on your gifts.

Pamela Slim
www.pamelaslim.com
TEDx Speaker, Entrepreneur,
Business Strategist and Award-Winning Author of 'Escape from Cubicle Nation' and 'Body of Work'.

HOW TO GET THE MOST OUT OF THIS BOOK

I sincerely believe that you will look at your career in two different parts:

Pre-*Unlock!*: your career before you read *Unlock!*

Post-*Unlock!*: your career after you read and implement *Unlock!*

This book will guide you through the 7 Step Process. Within each step, there are tools, templates, and activities.

In order to get the most out of this book, I recommend you keep the following in mind:

- The book is meant to be read in sequence to get the most value out of it.
- Feel free to come back to earlier parts of the book to reference.
- Use the QR code on the back cover of the book to download all the templates.
- Print these templates and use them with pen and paper. I know, old school. But there's something magical about putting pen to paper; it helps you think more deeply and puts more focus on the work that you are doing.
- Print multiple pages in case you need to rework some of these.

- For those of you who absolutely insist on using your computer, use the MS Office versions of the templates.
- Keep all documents in a folder for easy reference; we will refer to earlier work in parts of the book.
- The QR code also leads you to the free bonus features; take advantage of these as they work really well with *Unlock!* and help you further sharpen your leadership skills.
- **Pro tip:** Discuss the results of your exercises and the advice of this book in sessions with your friends, colleagues, mentors, and family. This is a great way to make sure you're getting feedback and support throughout this journey as you transform your career.

COMPLETE LIST OF UNLOCK! TOOLS

Unlock! Step	Tool/Framework
Mindset	Self-Awareness Exercise
	Skills Framework
	Market Framework
Step 1: North Star	North Star: Envisioned Future Tool
	North Star: Career Planning Tool
Step 2: Discovery	Discovery: Career Stack Tool
	Discovery: New Roles Tool
Step 3: Horizons	3 Horizons Tool
Step 4: Resolve	Decision Making Tool
	Commitment Tool
Step 5: Moniker	Hub & Spoke Strategy
	Elevator Pitch
Step 6: Elevate Leadership Flywheel	Leadership Flywheel
	ILPA Framework
	LIP Framework
	ACE Framework
	AMERIKA Framework
Step 7: Reinvent	Personal Performance Tracker

Purpose
Guides you toward self-awareness by collecting feedback from others.
Helps you identify your competencies and expertise and draw up a T-shaped skillset.
Helps you understand the different types of industry verticals and the functions within them to better review your market and reinvent your career.
Helps you imagine a future state where you are at your very best professionally and personally.
Helps you create a detailed career plan.
Helps you identify your skills and areas of experience to figure out your competencies.
Helps you design new roles and new titles for yourself depending on the competencies identified.
Helps you identify market trends so that you can take advantage of those trends and not get impacted by them.
Helps you make critical decisions by reviewing all available options.
Helps you identify and overcome any objections you have on acting on your decision.
Helps you craft a unique, consistent, online brand for yourself which enables others to engage with you on your ideas and concepts.
Is primarily a tool that helps you carry an engaging conversation about who you are.
Gives you compounded results and creates leadership opportunities for you.
Helps you create a game plan for the first 90 days of a new role.
Helps you be a better communicator.
Helps you understand your future opportunity better.
Helps you have great executive conversations for unlocking future opportunities.
Captures and tracks key pieces of information related to your performance.

TABLE OF CONTENTS

UNLOCK! FROM THE COVID19 SITUATION

"It was the best of times, it was the worst of times, it was the age of wisdom, it was the age of foolishness, it was the epoch of belief, it was the epoch of incredulity, it was the season of light, it was the season of darkness, it was the spring of hope, it was the winter of despair."

—Charles Dickens,
A Tale of Two Cities

"This too shall pass."

—Anonymous

Coronavirus. It is definitely the elephant in the room right now. How will this pandemic affect how we live, work, and play? What will be the immediate term and long-term consequences?

Answers to a lot of these questions will unravel over a period of time. But one thing is for certain: it is not going to be business as usual. The pandemic is going to bring in significant changes in our world, similar to other important events like World War II, the Fall of the Berlin Wall, 9/11, and the Great Financial Recession.

But this is not a time for doom and gloom. Every cataclysmic event like this one brings with it exceptional opportunities.

COVID19 has provided an exceptional opportunity for each one of us. For instance, it has given us time to reconnect with our family, our friends, and most importantly, ourselves. This transition from the daily treadmill of our intensely busy lives to one of quarantined self-isolation is an amazing silver lining to this cloud.

Let's take advantage of this amazing moment.

Use *Unlock!* to navigate the current situation and unlock the opportunities that lie beyond.

MARKET MECHANICS

An interplay between a global pandemic, oil prices, and an election year has created a market meltdown.

Markets are highly volatile with no end in sight. There is uncertainty, and as you know, markets hate uncertainty.

Corporate America is also not a fan of uncertainty, because it reduces visibility and creates challenges to forecast the business.

Companies are already starting to feel the heat. There will be pay cuts and even layoffs.

This situation is not the time to take it easy. It is time to be vigilant to protect your family, your community, your career, and your income.

WHEN WILL WE GET BACK TO "NORMAL"?

There are multiple factors that will determine when we come out of this; for example:

- Maintaining physical distancing
- Availability of testing and diagnosis
- Healthcare capacity
- Most importantly, creation and availability of a vaccine

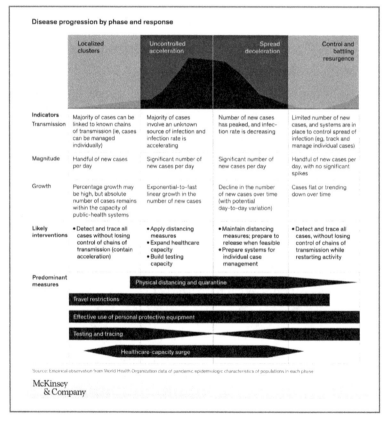

The above chart from McKinsey shows how the disease will likely progress and how we will be able to finally overcome it.

Here is the thing: even if we "overcome" the disease, we don't want a resurgence of it. That is why we will have to continue to do physical distancing. That is why we will not be getting back to "normal."

Our world has changed.

This is not a short-term change. It is creating new ways to live, and new ways to work. There will be winners, and there will be losers.

And I want you to be on the winning side.

HOW CAN I NAVIGATE THIS SITUATION?

There is absolutely a way to weather the storm and emerge in an even better shape after everything is said and done. From a career standpoint, we have the ability to face this and come out the other side much stronger, smarter and faster.

The answer lies in **Transformation.**

Unlock! provides seven essential steps to not only weather this storm, but to discover yourself in a new way, reimagine your career, and lead your way to leadership success.

This down time is a great time for self-reflection. It is a great opportunity to chart a new career path. To chart out a career path that is uniquely yours. A career path that excites you and energizes you. A career path that takes advantage of the market situation and rides on top of market trends. A career path that brings out the leader in you and puts you on the fast track toward leadership roles.

The question about your ability to produce results will be history when you put your full force behind your ability to learn & adapt!

SOURCE: WWW.NAPKINSIGHTS.COM/NAPKIN/863/

PART A

BECOMING A LEADER

Unlock! is about discovering yourself, tapping into your vast leadership potential, and creating meaning for the world.

People have amazing skills and virtually unlimited potential. But if you look closely at their career graph, there is usually a gap between its trajectory and their abilities. They are not engaged at work despite their ability to deliver high performance. This situation is clearly a disconnect between potential and performance.

This disconnect occurs because most of us have not made the "leadership switch," turning on that invisible switch that transforms us from merely working to leading successfully.

Unlock! is about leading yourself and others to create value and meaning in the world of business and technology.

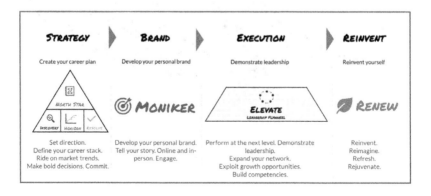

Unlock! is a set of seven steps that help you dig deeper and bring forth the successful leader you have the true potential to become. These steps are grouped together in four distinct parts of the 7 Step Process. Above is a quick view of the four parts; don't worry, we will go through each one of these together.

It is time to turn on the leadership switch. It is time to learn the steps, tools, and activities that will transform your career and help you realize your leadership potential. Let's start.

SOURCE: WWW.NAPKINSIGHTS.COM/NAPKIN/1045/

CHAPTER 1

THE LEADERSHIP SWITCH

According to the US Bureau of Labor Statistics, Americans spend eight hours and forty minutes on work- and work-related activities on a daily basis. This amount of time is more than time spent on any other activity including sleeping which is a little over seven hours on average.

Despite spending most of their time at work, Americans are disengaged while there. In fact, according to Gallup, about two-thirds (66 percent) of people in corporate America are not engaged[1].

That's interesting, isn't it? Most of us are disengaged in the activity we do the most. Every. Single. Day. This disengagement results in a career trajectory that is mediocre at best.

It's like investing all of your waking hours on diet and exercise but still becoming overweight. How counter intuitive!

That being said, each of us works hard. We have career aspirations.

---

1 Jim Harter, "Employee Engagement on the Rise in the US," Gallup, August 26, 2018, https://news.gallup.com/poll/241649/employee-engagement-rise.aspx

We absolutely intend to do better in our careers and create value for the world around us.

Over the years, I've had the opportunity to listen to people's career aspirations very closely. Usually, these career aspirations fit into ten categories. I am sure you will identify with one or more of these.

1. How can I become a successful leader, even if I'm stuck right now?
2. I want my career to be a rocket ship, but I don't have access to the right tools, guidance, or support to make that happen.
3. I want to take my job performance to the next level and get promoted to a role with more responsibilities.
4. I'd like to identify the latest market trends and ride those trends to better my career.
5. I want to build a personal brand and get known in my domain area / community.
6. I'm caught in an analysis-paralysis trap and can't figure out the way forward in my career.
7. I've been doing the same thing for many years, and I can't see myself getting out of this stagnation situation.
8. I want to reinvent myself, learn new things, and build a new personal brand.
9. I'm seeing people less qualified and less smart than I am get ahead; I want to figure out how to become successful in my work.
10. I want to figure out how to build a great professional network that will help me in the future.

As you read these, I am sure you can feel their importance and urgency. You can feel the yearning to break free of these problems, and the genuine desire to build a better career path.

If only they could *Unlock!* themselves.

Every single one of us has the potential to be a leader. Yes, we might not realize it, but all of us are destined to be leaders. A leader is anyone who moves others, influences others, drives others toward a higher achievement.

> There is absolutely a better career path for each of us. And that path is the way of the leader.

See, leadership is not a title; **leadership is action**. One can be a leader in any particular dimension, leader of a: particular topic, particular subject, process, domain, function, organization, group, or tribe.

Becoming a leader in any of these dimensions creates career growth opportunities. It helps us to take initiative and become accountable. It enables us to act as an owner rather than a "resource." It enables us to drive toward results and achieve goals. These achievements are not only for us as individuals but for the team, our organizations, and our communities.

Demonstrating leadership drives career growth. Yes, it is really that simple. Successful leadership is the journey and the destination.

However, most people are not able to demonstrate leadership and become successful leaders. It requires us to make the "leadership switch," turning on that invisible switch that moves us from merely working to leading successfully.

Unlock! gives you seven specific steps you can use to turn on that leadership switch. These steps help you unlock your potential to become a successful leader.

By the time you complete *Unlock*'s 7 Step Process, you will be able to unlock your potential and turn on the switch.

It is simple but not easy. It requires changing your mindset. It requires us to develop new capabilities which require personal investments. It is absolutely doable. The journey is exciting; there is never a dull moment. Guaranteed.

Turning on this "switch" unlocks your leadership potential to change your immediate future, and assists you for the rest of your life, professionally and personally. It is like learning to ride a bicycle. Or learning how to swim. Once you learn it, you will always carry it with you.

Ready? Excited? Let's jump in.

KEY TAKEAWAYS

- A leader is anyone who moves others, influences others, drives others toward a higher achievement.
- Leadership is not a title; leadership is action.
- Demonstrating leadership drives career growth.
- By the time you complete *Unlock*'s 7 Step Process, you will be able to unlock your potential and turn on the leadership switch.

CHAPTER 2

WHO SHOULD READ THIS BOOK?

Remember the last time you were in an exercise class? The instructor asks you to stretch. As you start stretching, it seems difficult. It feels a bit painful. As you ease into the stretch, it becomes easier and you start to enjoy it.

After the stretch, you feel refreshed. It feels like a caffeine shot for the body. Then you are ready to exercise more.

People who have used the steps, tools, and activities included in *Unlock!* have had similar experiences. They start with the steps; they may seem challenging at first. But as they get the hang of the process and use the activities and tools, working the process becomes easier. After going through the 7 Step Process, people are refreshed, recharged, and ready to take on the world.

You might wonder, "Is this book for me?" Let me share some thoughts on why this book could be for you.

- If you're ambitious, if you really want to tap into your leadership potential and reap more rewards, this book is for you.

- If you want to transform your career and put yourself on a much higher and faster career path, this book is for you.
- If you're frustrated that your ideas have not been working and, despite amazing work, you're not able to make progress in your projects, then this book is for you.
- If you're worried that your career has reached a dead end, and it's not going anywhere, and you're feeling depressed or disillusioned about your career progress, this book is for you.
- If you want to be known in your domain and in your community, and you really want to build a great personal brand, not only offline but also online, this book is for you.
- If you sense market trends that are going to become way bigger in the future, and you want to figure out how to take advantage of trends so they become tailwinds to drive you higher in your career trajectory, this book is for you.
- If you see people less qualified or less talented than you get ahead, and you want to understand how to catch up and move forward, this book is for you.
- If you want to figure out how to invest in a great career stack, build a great set of skills and experiences, and develop a fantastic professional network, then this book is for you.

INDIVIDUALS AND TEAMS CAN *UNLOCK!*

This book is ideal for professionals who want to transform themselves into truly successful leaders.

INDIVIDUAL PROFESSIONAL ⟶ SUCCESSFUL LEADER

This book is very helpful for managers who would like to build a really effective organization that has a high-performance leadership team.

TEAMS ➡ **EFFECTIVE ORGANIZATIONS**

KEY TAKEAWAYS

- *Unlock!* is ideal for professionals who want to transform themselves into truly successful leaders.
- It is also helpful for managers who would like to build a really effective organization that has a high-performance leadership team.

CHAPTER 3

THE JOURNEY IS THE DESTINATION

"Luck is where preparedness meets opportunity."

—Seneca

"The two most important days in your life are the day you are born and the day you find out why."

—Mark Twain

I came to the Bay Area in the '90s with a dream – to become a top programmer. Little did I know I would end up leading large-scale business transformations for the top tech companies on the planet. More on that later.

California in the late '90s was a place in the grips of dot com fever. With my programming skills, I knew I could make my mark as a great software coder.

I found myself working in San Francisco on one of the earliest online banking products. My job was to perform quality assurance (QA) for a whole bunch of software code. The code mapped banking processes to software functions that were written by an army of programmers. In today's terms, it was a fintech product. It was detail-oriented work; it was fulfilling and paid the bills.

Being new to the United States, I was itching to get a first-hand view of how corporate America worked. The ringside view was not enough; I wanted to be inside the ring.

But there was a problem. See, I was not "Career Rockstar" material. Not even close.

Here's what Career Rockstars have:

- Strong academic pedigree
- Phenomenal network
- Amazing personality

Even the lowest of the low Career Rockstars has at least one of these assets.

Here is what I had:

- My undergrad degree was, let's just say, from a rudimentary university. Far from Ivy League. Or any league.
- I had just moved to the United States, and I had zero network.
- Since I wasn't tall (I'm still not tall!) ☺ and have a face made for radio, I was never going to be mistaken for a charismatic leader.

It was depressing. The thought that I had nothing going for me created a dark emptiness that threatened to engulf my life. Imagine feeling weak and poor right in the home of democracy and capitalism.

It would have been easy to wallow in self-pity. But I've always prided myself in making the most out of available opportunities.

So, I made some promises to myself. I would:

- Work my tail off more than anyone else I know.
- Learn more about the industry and customers than anyone else.
- Learn soft skills, not just the required hard skills.
- Figure out how to create value for customers as well as for my team.
- Build a great professional network.

> You get lucky when preparation meets opportunity.

I took advantage of a strong job market to network and interview successfully with Deloitte, a premier management consulting firm. This was a strategic move that would enable me to learn how different companies and different industries worked in corporate America.

Remember my software QA skill set? I parlayed that experience into any management consultant's dream: business process re-engineering. These three words, at the intersection of business and technology, describe the necessary "last mile" work to ensure that large enterprises can automate processes and get the most out of their investments.

I served clients across the United States in many industries, ranging from energy, automotive, consumer, healthcare, pharma, to, of course, technology.

Thanks to a great firm and supportive colleagues, I was promoted twice and became a consulting manager. Instead of performing business process re-engineering, I was now leading business transformation engagements. Business transformation involves strategic work across multiple functions in the company. Which means more heavy-lifting and definitely more fulfilling work.

Management consulting in a Big 5 (now the Big 4) accounting firm was a great experience. However, it did have a major downside. Travel.

I was on a plane. A lot. Every. Single. Week.

With a growing family, I got weary of this traveling lifestyle. I quit to move to a local boutique consulting firm, Trianz. Here I was able to serve the local tech industry in Silicon Valley.

BECOMING A CONSULTING LEADER

While I was building my domain expertise in the tech industry at Trianz, one of the senior partners at Deloitte transferred to a large, public services firm: Cognizant. His charter was to start and establish a management consulting practice in a (predominantly) system integration company. He asked me to be part of his leadership team. I interviewed successfully with them and joined the party.

It was very entrepreneurial and exciting to build a brand-new management consulting practice from the ground up and serve clients around digital transformation. I helped technology companies figure out new business models at the intersection of cloud, analytics, mobile, and social.

I went from serving one client and handling one project model as an individual contributor to serving a client on multiple projects as a manager. In no time, I was serving multiple clients on multiple projects as a leader. In consulting terminology, I became a consulting principal aka "partner".

That is how I became a leader in the tech industry:

- Focusing on client value
- Developing T-shaped domain skills
- Having a great work ethic
- Exceeding expectations
- Telling my story effectively
- Building a great network[2]

These practices and approach became my playbook for a successful career. The playbook was indeed working. I was about to discover a critical element for my career playbook: taking advantage of market disruption.

In 2011, Marc Andreesen came out with his seminal essay, "Why Software Is Eating the World."

At that time, he argued that every major industry was going to be transformed because of software. "Companies in every industry need to assume that a software revolution is coming," he said. It was a prescient observation. Andreesen's hypothesis has been proven. Every industry from transportation, manufacturing, and healthcare to education as well as many others are undergoing digital transformation[3].

As I was helping multiple tech clients in the SaaS and cloud space, it became very clear that this industry was about to blow up. In a good way! Management consulting was always dear to me, but I wanted to get more skin in the game, especially in tech.

In 2013, one of my clients at Cisco recruited me into their leadership

---

2 The tools that I used for my success are covered in the book in detail.

3 Marc Andreesen, "Why Software is Eating the World," https://www.wsj.com/articles/SB10 001424053111903480904576512250915629460, *Wall Street Journal*, August 11, 2011. *TechCrunch* followed up with another article in 2016, "Software Is Still Eating the World."

team to focus on customer experience and monetization. That experience turned out to be way better than expected.

My management consulting experience driving large scale change combined with SaaS domain expertise came in real handy.

That is how one gets lucky: when preparation meets opportunity.

I was in the eye of the storm. Breaking glass every day. Learning new things. Driving critical transformations that drove incremental revenue measured in $B not $M.

This journey created even more opportunities for me personally and professionally:

- Exposure to products across some of the most cutting-edge technologies: SaaS (Webex, AppDynamics), cloud (Meraki), security, and the internet of things (IoT).
- Experience in developing business models, pricing, and go-to-market plans at global scale.
- Product management experience to drive AI and analytics features based on data points gathered from millions of connected devices.
- Involvement in the guts of incubating customer success and a digital experience for hundreds of customers.

It was clear that the cloud and SaaS wave was here to stay.

In fact, Gartner's 2019 cloud report[4] shows that SaaS will continue to grow at 20 percent.

---

4 'Gartner Forecasts Worldwide Public Cloud Revenue to Grow 17.5 Percent in 2019,' Gartner Press Release, April 2, 2019, https://www.gartner.com/en/newsroom/press-releases/2019-04-02-gartner-forecasts-worldwide-public-cloud-revenue-to-g.

TABLE 1. WORLDWIDE PUBLIC CLOUD SERVICE REVENUE FORECAST (BILLIONS OF U.S. DOLLARS)

	2018	2019	2020	2021	2022
Cloud Business Process Services (BPaaS)	45.8	49.3	53.1	57.0	61.1
Cloud Application Infrastructure Services (PaaS)	15.6	19.0	23.0	27.5	31.8
Cloud Application Services (SaaS)	80.0	94.8	110.5	126.7	143.7
Cloud Management and Security Services	10.5	12.2	14.1	16.0	17.9
Cloud System Infrastructure Services (IaaS)	30.5	38.9	49.1	61.9	76.6
TOTAL MARKET	**182.4**	**214.3**	**249.8**	**289.1**	**331.2**

BPaaS = business process as a service; IaaS = infrastructure as a service; PaaS = platform as a service; SaaS = software as a service
Note: Totals may not add up due to rounding.

Identifying market trends is critical to career moves. Realizing the market was trending toward customer experience expertise in a major way, I made my move from Cisco to a new SaaS entrepreneurial opportunity, enterpriseCX. In this new role, I am helping enterprises and SaaS companies create more customer value and drive subscription growth.

And I am always learning.

ALWAYS LEARNING

In my journey so far, I have learned much from my mentors and my network. There are people who don't even know I have learned from them. This book is a way for me to pay it forward so others will be able to learn the tools and techniques to unlock career potential and elevate themselves to be leaders.

THE NETWORK EFFECT

Every single career opportunity that came to me was through my network.

It is so important to build and nurture our networks so we can create value for others, and also so others can create value for us.

THE RELUCTANT LEADERSHIP COACH

I've always been passionate about helping professionals, both in my network and out of it.

In 2009, in the midst of financial recession, I started helping out some friends with their job search. They were successfully hired despite an unbelievably tough market. Then they told their friends. Soon, my phone was ringing with requests from complete strangers. As I coached more people, I was featured in newspapers, magazines, and online media.

Assisting others with their careers wasn't restricted to off-work hours. In my leadership roles, I always pride myself in being available as a coach and mentor to my team members and people in other functions in the broader company. Yep, anyone from marketing, sales, product, operations, supply chain, HR, or IT would request my time.

For ten plus years, I've had the good fortune of helping thousands of people with advice, mentorship, and access to resources.

But something was wrong. *Extremely* wrong.

The truth is, I never wanted to be a career coach or a leadership coach. I was concerned about how much this coaching work was eating into my personal time.

There were many voices in my head, and one of those voices was saying, "I am the quintessential technology business leader with products to build and markets to capture. Why the *bleep* am I spending time and energy with so many folks?"

I struggled with this for a long time. I couldn't say no to them because they needed my help. My empathetic side always won over the dark side. I obliged and made time for coaching others.

I finally found the answer.

By serving others, and helping them become successful leaders, I was becoming a better leader.

I had accidently discovered **servant leadership**.

And this continues till today; complete strangers email me or call me for help. I answer that call. Because by answering that call, I'm helping myself.

> By serving others, and helping them
> to become successful leaders,
> I was becoming a better leader.

It may seem like cognitive dissonance, but by helping others, I am selfishly helping myself.

The playbook and tools I had used for myself, are now being used to help others. They are included in this book.

> **KEY TAKEAWAYS**
> - You get lucky when preparation meets opportunity.
> - It is important to build and nurture your networks to create value for others and also for them to create value for you.
> - By serving others, and helping them become successful leaders, you can become a better leader.

CHAPTER 4

WHY DO I WANT YOU TO HAVE A LEADERSHIP CAREER?

"Leadership is an opportunity to serve."

—J Donald Walters

YOUR CAREER IS YOUR RESPONSIBILITY

It is getting close to 10:00 a.m. on May 16, 2019. My hands are clammy, and my nose is twitchy. It is late spring in Northern California. It can't be allergies, I've already taken my non-drowsy anti-allergic medication. It's probably nerves.

It is the first video interview of the Career Nation Show[5], with Sheila Jordan. If you haven't heard about Sheila, you should. She is the Chief Digital Technology Officer at Honeywell and former Chief Information Officer at Symantec®, one of the world's leading security software companies. She is also a board member at Slack. In other words, she is a fearless female leader in the tech industry,

---

5 Career Nation Show, https://podcasts.apple.com/us/podcast/career-nation-show/id1467151401

which is notorious for low gender diversity[6].

I try to hide my nervousness as the interview starts. I think I'm being successful at it as we get into the discussion.

And then Sheila launches into a prophetic message, "Don't give your career to your manager, to your environment, to your work, to someone else. Don't be a victim of your career. You own it; you get to decide what you want to do, what you want to be, where you work; you own that."

That's it! My career is my responsibility. I'd always been convinced of this deep down, but it was not until Sheila articulated it that it became so clear.

THIS IS AN EMERGENCY

You could outsource your travel by calling an Uber. Get dinner by ordering via DoorDash or GrubHub. Or get groceries delivered.

Is it possible to do the same for exercising? Obviously not! You have to put in the work to stay fit and healthy.

What about your career growth? Can someone else do it for you?

Nope! Your career growth is your job #1. And guess what? You have to put in the work yourself.

No cavalry is going to show up to help you. Your company might provide adequate resources, but it is not going to help you drive your career. Your manager might offer you some advice based on their vantage point, but it's not going to replace your effort and accountability.

---

6 Blanka Myers, "Women and Minorities in Tech, By the Numbers," Wired, March 27, 2018, https://www.wired.com/story/computer-science-graduates-diversity/.

You are responsible. You are accountable. For your life's sake.

That's why taking control of your career right now is an emergency. Every day you put it off, you are moving away from having a great career and a better life. It's like you are digging your own grave. It is time to stop digging and take control of your career.

WHO IS A LEADER?

Everyone has the capability to be a leader. Anyone can be a leader.

Leadership is not a title. It is not about having a title.

A leader is anyone who leads a collection of individuals toward a goal or outcome.

You are a leader if you lead a:

1. Process
2. Goal
3. Topic
4. Event
5. Function
6. Outcome
7. Team
8. Project
9. Association or a group
10. Customer / vendor / partner

If you lead any of these, or if you can make the effort to lead any of these, you are a leader. Period. End of story.

IS LEADERSHIP A LOT OF WORK?

When you were learning to ride a bike, it took a lot of effort. Maybe one of your parents or grandparents or close family helped you to learn. As you learned more, you gained confidence. After some time, riding became second nature. Now, you don't even think twice about hopping on. It comes naturally to you and it is effortless.

Leadership is very similar.

You might have to put some effort into it initially, and get help from others, including mentors, teachers, and coaches. Over a period of time, you will surely master it.

Once you make the leadership switch, it comes naturally to you. It is effortless.

FOOD IN THE FRIDGE: WHY I WANT YOU TO HAVE A LEADERSHIP CAREER

In corporate America, there is an unwritten mantra: up or out.

You can have a trajectory that is upward: better skills, more experience, better titles, and higher responsibilities. Or you can be moved out of your job to a different one or asked to leave.

You see, there is no middle ground. There is a section of people that want to "coast" in their jobs, which is another name for doing the bare minimum required for the job to collect compensation and benefits.

Sorry folks, coasting is a dead end. As companies optimize their teams, their workloads, and look at different ways of getting work done, coasting is dead. At some point, your manager or your company will find out. People who want to coast along in their jobs either leave on their own or are categorized in the "out" category.

It is like food in the fridge. Not good enough to eat. Not bad enough to throw in the trash. It just sits there. Until it is really time to throw it out.

Don't be food in the fridge.

When you have a leadership trajectory, you create outcomes, deliver results, and manifest value. You:

- Leverage your strengths
- Help others
- Create more value
- Gain visibility
- Receive higher compensation
- And get promoted

And that is why my sincere wish for you is to take up the mantle of a leader.

Opportunity awaits.

TALK IS CHEAP: SHOULD YOU LISTEN TO ARMCHAIR EXPERTS?

You know the type: this person will claim to have all the experience and knowledge in the world. But he doesn't. The guy has never been a leader in the corporate world. Nor has he ever had the scars on his back that teach real world lessons. However, he will talk a great talk. You might have heard this type of career advice a million times.

"Follow your passion."

Or ...

"Do a great job and everything will follow."

Or ...

"Work hard, play hard."

... And many more.

These are sound bites that typically surface during work conversations. The advice feels good, but it is not actionable at all.

People who give this type of advice are generally good-natured people who themselves might not know what they are talking about. These are armchair experts.

And they are everywhere. In fact, you might have already come across some of them. The reason armchair experts exist is because career advice is easy to give. Talk is cheap.

See, career advice is easy to give, but it's very hard to implement because often there are bigger questions behind these clichéd answers.

- What should I pursue from a career standpoint? What should be my objective and goals?
- How do I know what my passion is? Should I follow my passion?
- How can I become a successful leader?
- How can I demonstrate leadership?
- How can I create value? Not only for myself but also for my organization and my community?
- What does it mean to do a great job? Isn't that a relative term?
- I understand I should work hard and put in the effort. But in what areas? Where should I invest my time and energy?
- Why is option A better than option B for my career? Why do I feel so strongly about a particular career path vs another? Where does my true expertise lie?
- What should be my next career move? What kind of investment will be required? What tools can I use to move ahead?
- Have my career choices been effective so far? Why? Why not?

These are questions for which we do not get satisfactory answers from armchair experts.

You Google for solutions or seek career advice from friends, colleagues, or managers, but you do not find answers to your specific questions and your specific situation. You do get advice, but it is fairly generic, and it is hard to apply generic advice to your specific situation.

WHY I MENTOR OTHERS, AND WHY I WROTE THIS BOOK

I have observed people in various industries, in different companies and roles struggle to find ways to transform their career. They are talented, smart, and hardworking people, but unable improve the course of their professional lives.

I saw this pain and frustration firsthand. So much great talent and potential was not being fulfilled. If people could *Unlock!* this potential, they could not only help themselves but also help the people, organizations, and communities around them. Talk about a win-win-win. I found it meaningful to help colleagues and industry peers with their careers.

It created meaning for me.

That is why I wanted to solve this problem of career frustration and stagnation: help these smart, hard-working professionals realize their true potential, to realize their dreams and aspirations.

Over the course of my career journey, I developed approaches and tools for advancement. Some of those tools became super clear to me immediately, and some were developed over a period of time.

During my experiences in the corporate world and my coaching practice, I used these tools to help hundreds of professionals. They not only liked using these tools, but by applying them, they found success in a variety of areas: getting promoted, finding better opportunities, identifying new ventures, or building high performance teams. You, too, can find the same success.

These tools are now available to develop your own career and become a successful leader.

YOUR UNIQUE CAREER PATH

Have you seen yourself in the mirror lately? If you haven't checked recently, please do it now.

I'll wait.

You might have noticed that you are unique on the planet. There is no one else who looks exactly like you, has the same first name, has the same family members, has lived in the same places, has experienced the exact same journey ... you get the idea.

Your career journey is uniquely yours. It will be a unique career path based on your potential, your skills, and your experience.

This is how *Unlock!* helps you: it provides tools for you to succeed in your own, unique career journey.

UNLOCK! THE INSIDE STORY

By now, you know my story, right? I literally had nothing going for me. As I went through the darkest of my days, I considered how I could build a great career despite the adversity. How could I take advantage of market trends? How could I get into a great job opportunity? And most importantly, how could I make this success repeatable and sustainable?

I used to doodle a lot. (Still do!) I used visuals to express the solutions to my career problem. These visuals became a way for me to solve specific problems: career direction, finding my next job, improving my performance. These visuals became my tools and the basis for my playbook.

And thanks to those tools and resultant playbook, I was able to chart out a successful career with roles across the following industries and functions over the last twenty years.

1. **Industries:** tech, financial services, healthcare, life sciences, manufacturing, media, and energy
2. **Functions:** marketing, sales, product, services, supply chain, operations, and IT
3. **Technologies:** cloud, SaaS stack, CRM, marketing automation, sales automation, service automation, data analytics, and AI

In the last ten years or so, I've been actively coaching professionals in Silicon Valley and beyond. As I coached these amazing individuals across companies, industries, and functions, I observed where they were getting stuck and identified specific patterns.

I discovered that the tools that had helped me in my own career were not only applicable to others but also created amazing results for them. By using these tools in coaching sessions over a period of time, they have become sharper, polished, refined, and effective.

And now, these tools are available to you. Let's explore them and apply them to transform your career and realize your true leadership potential.

KEY TAKEAWAYS

- Your career growth is your job #1.
- A leader is anyone who leads a collection of individuals toward a goal or outcome.
- When you have a leadership trajectory, you create outcomes, deliver results, and manifest value.

CHAPTER 5

7 STEPS TO *UNLOCK!*

"Congratulations!
Today is your day.
You're off to Great Places!
You're off and away!

You have brains in your head.
You have feet in your shoes.
You can steer yourself
Any direction you choose."

— Dr. Seuss, *Oh, the Places You'll Go!*

Think of *Unlock!* as a toolbox that you can always carry around with you. In a toolbox, there are different places to put your **tools**: flathead screwdrivers in one compartment, Phillips screwdrivers in another. In *Unlock!* there are also compartments that we call **steps** to contain your tools. In addition, a toolbox may have different drawers. The first drawer may contain all your screwdrivers, the second all your hammers, etc. *Unlock!* also has drawers that we call **parts** of our process. There are four parts: Strategy, Brand, Execution, and Reinvent.

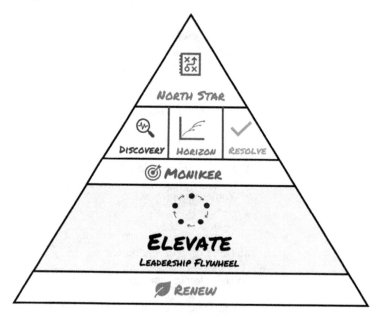

7 Steps to Unlock!

Let me introduce you to the 7 Step Process:

1. **North Star**: develop career strategy and planning
2. **Discovery**: identify your skills and discover new career opportunities
3. **Horizon**: ride on market trends
4. **Resolve**: make bold career decisions and commit to them
5. **Moniker**: develop your personal brand
6. **Elevate Leadership Flywheel**: demonstrate leadership
7. **Renew**: reinvent yourself

Let's learn a bit more about the features of each step.

1. NORTH STAR

The first part of the 7 Step Process is the **North Star** Step. Just like navigating using the real **North Star**, you can constantly check your current position against the **North Star**'s location to make sure you are maintaining your set course. This step helps you create a strategy and a plan to set your course for your personal **North Star**. The step helps you build on your strengths and learn continuously so you keep moving forward at a steady pace.

2. DISCOVERY

The **Discovery Step** provides the opportunity to uncover potential new roles and identify your skills to open doors to new opportunities. At the end of the **Discovery Step**, you will be able to package your skills and experience in new, interesting ways as preparation for exploring new roles and career opportunities based on your current career path, skills, and interests. This step is also useful for professionals looking to reinvent and reboot their careers.

3. HORIZON

Career opportunities are determined by the market. Supply and demand trends determine which skills become more valuable or less valuable over time. The **Horizon Step** helps you analyze market trends to figure out how to plan your career moves. This step helps you take advantage of market trends rather than being impacted by them.

4. RESOLVE

Sometimes, it is easy to get stuck in the thinking process which could result in analysis-paralysis: lots of thoughts, ideas, and plans, but no action. This inaction becomes a roadblock that prevents translation of a great plan into reality. The **Resolve Step** helps you make clear, well informed decisions, remove roadblocks, and commit yourself to executing the plan. It jumpstarts you from just having a plan to making real progress.

5. MONIKER

The ability to tell your story effectively, engage others, and demonstrate a great personal brand is critical to leadership success. The **Moniker Step** helps you develop your personal brand. This step shows you how to demonstrate executive presence using social media tools as well as in person.

6. ELEVATE

The **Elevate Step** puts the Leadership Flywheel in motion. The Leadership Flywheel is a set of activities designed to create massive results over a period of time due to a "compounding" effect. You become a BETTER leader and take your career to the next level. Each activity on the flywheel automatically leads to the next, and that is how you build momentum, continuously building your leadership skills and accelerating your career growth.

You can see a quick snapshot of the Elevate Leadership Flywheel in the next page.

Build competencies: While on the job, you have many opportunities to build new skills, gain new experiences, and upgrade your competency to adapt to the emerging changes in the market.

Exceed expectations: From the time you start your job, you begin an ongoing journey of doing great work by building strong relationships with your peers and superiors, creating value for others, exceeding expectations consistently, and demonstrating leadership skills in the process.

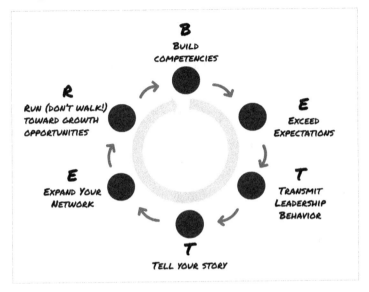

Elevate Leadership Flywheel

Transmit leadership behavior: In order to be seen as a leader, you need to understand key leadership traits and demonstrate leadership performance at your current level or the next level.

Tell your story: The great work that you do must be shared. Learn to tell your story effectively to connect and engage with your network.

Expand your network: Expand your network to include more contacts, domains, and diversity. Connect, engage, and activate your network.

Run (don't walk) toward growth opportunities: Expanding your network leads you toward growth opportunities. Understand how to capitalize on these opportunities.

7. REINVENT

At the very end of the 7 Steps Process is the **Reinvent Step**. This includes time to check in with yourself to see where you are in your career, review what you would like to do next, and reinvent yourself in preparation for that next step. The **Reinvent Step** helps you to make career moves in tune with the market and stay relevant.

HOW DO THE 7 STEPS WORK TOGETHER?

We are going to be following four phases that lead us to the goal of career transformation and leadership success.

1. **Strategy:** Create career strategy using the **North Star, Discovery, Horizon,** and **Resolve Steps.** Learn how to create a strategy that leverages your skillset, helps you take advantage of market trends, and allows you to make critical career decisions.

2. **Brand:** Leverage your career strategy to develop a great personal brand using the **Moniker Step.** Learn how to build your brand using online social media tools as well as offline experiences, i.e. in person.

3. **Execution:** A great strategy with no execution is a hallucination. The **Execution Step** with its Elevate Leadership Flywheel puts your strategy and brand in motion. It is only through execution that you will demonstrate leadership and get compounding success.

4. **Reinvent:** Our world is changing rapidly around us and the **Reinvent Step** gives you the opportunity to reflect on your work and life thus far and determine how to reinvent yourself for the future.

HOW TO USE THE *UNLOCK!* 7 STEP PROCESS

As you can see, there are four phases to the 7 Step Process. The steps are contained within those phases. Within each step, there are tools, templates, and activities. In order to get the best benefit from the book, we have made some of these tools and templates available to you. To get these, you can:

- Use the templates in the book.
- Use the QR code on the back cover of the book to download templates. Then do one of the following:
    - For those of you who absolutely insist on using your computer, use these downloaded files.
    - Print these templates out and use them with pen and paper. I know, old school. There's something magical about putting pen to paper; it helps you think more deeply and puts more focus on the work that you are doing. Print multiple pages as you might have to rework some of these.

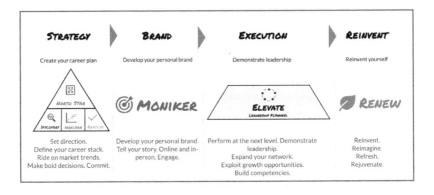

Pro tip: Discuss the results of your exercises and the advice of this book in sessions with your friends, colleagues, mentors, and family. This is a great way to make sure you're getting feedback and support throughout this journey as you transform your career.

As you know, a great journey requires preparation.

Before we get into each of the steps and their associated tools and exercises, make sure that you have oriented yourself in the right way.

In the next section, you'll familiarize yourself with the terminology, building blocks, and mindset required for this journey.

KEY TAKEAWAYS

- *Unlock!* gives you the tools for career success through the seven steps: North Star, Discovery, Horizon, Resolve, Moniker, Elevate Leadership Flywheel, and Renew.
- *Unlock!* is a toolbox that you can always carry around with you.

PART B

PREPARATION

"The more you sweat in peace, the less you bleed in war."

—Gen. Norman Schwarzkopf

To best prepare for career transformation, take a step back and invest some time to prepare yourself for these changes. Preparation is an important prelude to the process and empowers you with clarity, focus, and information for the task ahead.

In this preparation section, we will discuss the following topics to get your ready for the *Unlock!* 7 Step Process:

- Ikigai: defining the purpose-driven leader
- Why leadership is not a title
- How to develop the necessary mindset
- How to develop self-awareness to analyze your positives and negatives
- How to double down on your strengths and get better at what you do
- What T-shaped skills are and how to get them

- How to analyze the market and find the most suitable roles in the most suitable verticals

Once you finish the preparation section, you will be well-equipped to delve into the strategy section and start your journey of career transformation.

THE FIRST STEP IN THE PURSUIT OF A PRIZE IS TO FALL IN LOVE WITH THE PREPARATION TO GET THERE!

PREPARATION IS PRICELESS

SOURCE: WWW.NAPKINSIGHTS.COM/NAPKIN/76/

CHAPTER 6

IKIGAI: THE PURPOSE-DRIVEN LEADER

A career is more than making money. Ideally, a career should be fueled by a mission, a purpose.

Working with a purpose helps leaders generate the energy and excitement required to overcome adversity and ensure success.

It is important to establish coherence between values, interests, skills, and income.

The framework that can help bind these together and establish coherence is Ikigai.

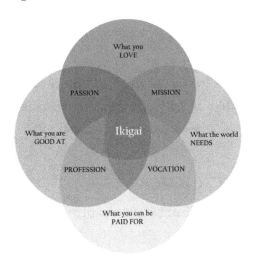

In Okinawa, Japan, Ikigai is thought of as a reason to get up in the morning, which also means living life with a purpose. This concept is instrumental in your growth because it really helps you develop intention in your personal and professional life.

To come up with your Ikigai, you need to populate the four circles that are displayed in this picture. You can leverage the four essential questions in the outside circles to inform this framework. Let's go counter-clockwise on this picture.

#1 is What do you love? What do you love to do? What are the things you really like? What are you passionate about?

#2 is What are you good at? Are there certain skills or competencies at which you're really adept?

#3 is What can you get paid for? What type of work pays top dollar?

#4 is What does the world need from you? This question is critical. How can you create value for the world? How can you help the communities and people who are important to you?

As you come up with the answers to these questions, feel free to add those responses to each circle. Don't worry much about the number of words or phrases or grammar. Do your best to dig deep and come up with as many words or phrases as you can for each of these circles.

As you populate this information in different circles, the circles start to intersect. Within all the pieces of information in those circles, you will find a pattern, thread, or even several patterns.

For example:

#1 What do you love: financial analysis

#2 What are you good at: I'm great with numbers.

#3 What can you get paid for: telling a business story with numbers

#4 What does the world need from you: sharing analysis and insights to help customers make better buying decisions

As you populate the information and find these patterns, it will lead to intersections of these four circles. These intersections take you closer to Ikigai: the final intersection where all circles meet.

The ideal career choice for you is at the intersection of the four circles:

- You really love that work.
- You're really good at it.
- This is something that the world needs from you.
- You'll get paid well for it.

And once you find that career, you can move mountains because you are living a life filled with purpose.

Truth be told, it takes time and effort to go through this exercise. However, going through this exercise helps a person think deeply and find their purpose, their mission. Once you discover that, you will be on your way toward a purposeful career and a fulfilling life.

KEY TAKEAWAYS

- Working with a purpose helps leaders generate the energy and excitement required to overcome adversity and ensure success.
- Ikigai is a Japanese framework that helps bind value, interests, skills, and income together.

CHAPTER 7

LEADERSHIP IS NOT A TITLE

As we saw in chapter four, leadership is not necessarily a title. A leader is anyone who leads a collection of individuals toward a goal or outcome. You are a leader if you lead a process, a topic, a function, an organization, etc.

In fact, **leadership is action.**

Leadership is about taking action that creates value, produces an outcome, or solves a problem.

As you go through your personal journey of becoming a successful leader, keep these key leadership characteristics in mind:

1. **Authentic:** Leaders are true to themselves; they do not put on a "show." They are authentic in their behavior. They do not create different personas at work and outside of work. They are sincere and loyal.

2. **Learning and growth mindset:** Leaders like to learn continuously. They are not ashamed to admit they don't know something and are always looking for opportunities to learn. Satya Nadella famously said, "I'd rather hire a learn-it-all than a know-it-all."

A great reference here is Carol Dweck's growth mindset[7].

3. **Empathy and passion to create value:** Leaders create an empathy muscle which allows them to understand what it's like to walk in the other person's shoes. Once they identify with someone else's problems and pain, they develop a passion to solve the problems and take away the pain. When empathy and passion go hand in hand, it creates momentum toward action and problem solving.

4. **Culture:** Leaders demonstrate good values and culture, not only through their words but more importantly their actions.

5. **Decisiveness and value-based decisions:** Leaders have a bias toward making decisions. Sometimes one may not have enough data to make a decision. Here is where Jeff Bezos' Type 1 and Type 2 frameworks come in handy.

   - Type 1 decisions are not reversible, and you have to be very careful making them.
   - Type 2 decisions are like walking through a door. If you don't like the decision, you can always go back.
   - If it's a Type 2 decision, leaders can be decisive to move forward. A Type 1 decision will require more due diligence since it is not reversible.

6. **Own it!:** Leaders have a sense of ownership and they demonstrate that in their day-to-day actions. Leaders act as an owner to take responsibility for problems. Or they own the customer by making sure that the customer has everything he/she needs to be successful. They might also own the project to ensure the success of the project.

---

7 Carol Dweck, "The Power of Believing You Can Improve," Ted Talks, November 2014, https://www.ted.com/talks/carol_dweck_the_power_of_believing_that_you_can_improve.

7. **Guiding the team:** Leaders develop a coaching habit to work with team members, peers, and stakeholders. This involves not just providing solutions all the time but also asking the right questions to support team members develop solutions.

8. **Fun to be with:** Leaders are fun to be around and hang out with. They are great listeners, and tell stories, often interlaced with humor.

Keep these leadership characteristics in mind when you create your career plan in the **North Star Step.**

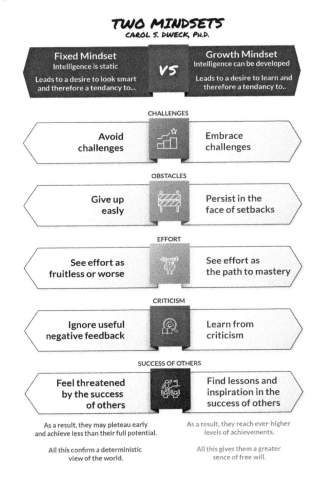

TWO MINDSETS
CAROL S. DWECK, PH.D.

Fixed Mindset		Growth Mindset
Intelligence is static	**VS**	Intelligence can be developed
Leads to a desire to look smart and therefore a tendancy to...		Leads to a desire to learn and therefore a tendancy to..

CHALLENGES
| Avoid challenges | | Embrace challenges |

OBSTACLES
| Give up easly | | Persist in the face of setbacks |

EFFORT
| See effort as fruitless or worse | | See effort as the path to mastery |

CRITICISM
| Ignore useful negative feedback | | Learn from criticism |

SUCCESS OF OTHERS
| Feel threatened by the success of others | | Find lessons and inspiration in the success of others |

| As a result, they may pleteau early and achieve less than their full potential. | As a result, they reach ever-higher levels of achievements. |
| All this confirm a deterministic view of the world. | All this gives them a greater sence of free will. |

KEY TAKEAWAYS

- Leaders are sincere, loyal, and above all, true to themselves.
- Leaders always have a learning and growth mindset.
- Leaders are empathetic and understand where the other person is coming from.
- Leaders are decisive and have a sense of ownership.
- Leaders are mentors who guide their peers and team members.

CHAPTER 8

CAUTION, MINDSET SHIFT REQUIRED

"Neo, sooner or later you're going to realize just as I did that there's a difference between knowing the path and walking the path."

—Morpheus, *The Matrix*

I wish I could tell you that this journey is going to be easy. I can't. But I will certainly promise that it will be exciting and worth the effort. Every step, no matter how small or large, that you make toward implementing these strategies and tools will transform your leadership capabilities.

SPEED OF ACTION

"If everything's under control, you're going too slow."

—Robin S. Sharma, *The Leader Who Had No Title*[8]

Speed is the currency of business. Moving fast and having a bias for

---

8. Sharma, Robin, *The Leader Who Had No Title: A Modern Fable on Real Success in Business and in Life* (Free Press, 2010, ISBN: 978-1439109137)

action is essential. In the immediate term, having a bias for action gets things done and moving along in the right direction. Diametrically opposite to that is having the patience to bide your time for the right opportunities.

It will essentially boil down to this: if you are waiting for all the stars to align and all conditions to be perfect for you to start anything, you will never start. The key to action is to start even if there are unfavorable conditions.

TURN PROBLEMS INTO OPPORTUNITIES, NOT EXCUSES

A problem is an opportunity in disguise. In fact, it is a gift. But since the wrapper of a problem is painful and unpleasant, many people do not care to unwrap the gift. Run toward problems, and not away from them. Believe you will be able to figure out how to overcome the obstacle, and this approach will help you solve it sooner and more decisively.

> It is guaranteed there will be some setbacks and failures on the path to success, and our approach to handling those makes all the difference.

OVERCOME RESISTANCE AND PUT IN THE WORK

For many people, leadership and a great career are distant dreams. They have great ideas, great plans, and even great networks to potentially manifest an amazing career journey.

But they have a gap. They do not put in the work because they face resistance.

Steven Pressfield has articulated the term resistance in his seminal work, *The War of Art*[9]. (Not to be confused with Sun Tzu's *The Art of War*).

> *"Most of us have two lives. The life we live, and the unlived life within us. Between the two stands Resistance.*
>
> *Resistance is the most toxic force on the planet. It is the root of more unhappiness than poverty, disease, and erectile dysfunction. To yield to Resistance deforms our spirit.*
>
> *Resistance cannot be seen, touched, heard, or smelled. But it can be felt. We experience it as an energy field radiating from a work-in-potential. It's a repelling force. It's negative. Its aim is to shove us away, distract us, prevent us from doing our work."*

When you are giving yourself excuses to put off important work, it is resistance in action. If you feel like procrastinating, it is resistance at work.

In fact, resistance becomes even more powerful when the work is critical to our success. "Rule of thumb: the more important a call or action is to our soul's evolution, the more Resistance we will feel toward pursuing it," Pressfield says.

How do we beat resistance?

Pressfield offers a simple solution – turn professional. Note that I mentioned simple but not easy. ☺ Here is how Pressfield describes what "turning professional" means.

---

9.   Pressfield, Steven, *The War of Art: Break Through the Blocks and Win Your Inner Creative Battles* (Black Irish Entertainment, LLC, 2012, ISBN: 978-1936891023)

We show up every day.

We show up no matter what.

We stay on the job all day.

We are committed over the long haul.

The stakes for us are high and real.

We accept remuneration for our labor.

We do not over-identify with our jobs.

We master the technique of our jobs.

We have a sense of humor about our jobs.

We receive praise or blame in the real world.

There will be highs and lows as you apply the strategies and tools. Turning professional is the way to beat the resistance. We have to do it every day, because unfortunately resistance shows up every day. For each and every one of us.

KEY TAKEAWAYS

- Resistance becomes more powerful when the work is critical to our success.
- To beat resistance, turn professional.

CHAPTER 9

DO YOU KNOW WHO YOU ARE?

"You will start finding opportunities once you become self-aware."

—Rajesh Setty

"Figure out who you are. Optimize who you are. But never apologize for who you are. Ever. Self-awareness at its finest, is accepting your shortcomings and accentuating your strengths."

—Gary Vaynerchuck

L eadership starts with self-awareness.

It is an essential step to become aware of yourself: your skills, your experience, your strengths, and your weaknesses. This is the building block as we get into skills, experience, career strategy, and career planning.

Self-awareness is all about knowing ourselves, or as the Greeks said, "Know thyself." It's about understanding your own thoughts, your emotions, your skills, your experiences, your desires, your strengths, and your weaknesses. It's about being very candid and very honest – even brutally honest – with yourself.

In my own experience, some of the most pointed feedback I've received in these self-awareness sessions has helped me avoid so much pain and so many years of agony.

Performing a self-awareness exercise and developing a self-awareness muscle are essential to career transformation. If you fail to do that, you will put your career at risk.

Fundamentally, there are two ways to develop self-awareness: one way is to get help from others, and the other is to do it yourself.

SELF-AWARENESS EXERCISE: GETTING HELP FROM OTHERS

Getting help from others is all about getting together with your friends, your family, and your close colleagues to discuss "you."

It is recommended that you include people you trust in this list:

- Friends
- Current and former colleagues and peers
- Former managers (very important!) and current manager if you are comfortable with them
- Your spouse (I know, this could escalate quickly.)
- Current or former customers and stakeholders

Here's the process for the self-awareness exercise:

1. Ask for a one-on-one meeting with your spouse, partner, close friend, or a colleague.

2. **Very important:** Thank them and make sure you let them know that this exercise is going to help you a lot. Let them know that you are looking for objective feedback, and there will be no ill feelings or negative repercussions from this conversation, and that your relationship will not be affected because of this exercise.

3. Tell them that you really want to understand your strengths and weaknesses. What are the things you're really good at, and where do you need more improvement? You can ask them to list their responses in no particular order.

4. As they share this information, take a ton of notes. You could also record this as audio. (But make sure to ask for the person's permission.)

5   **Very important:** Just take it all in while not exercising any judgment. DO NOT show any emotion. Do not try to counter any feedback you are getting. You would be surprised at the amount of information you get.

6. After they are done sharing feedback, be sure to keep asking the question, "What else would you like to share?" Ask this question multiple times. I'm always surprised by how people open up even more when a question is asked a few times.

7. Thank the participant. You can show gratitude by offering to pay for lunch or coffee. Or send them a gift.

8. With this meeting still fresh in your mind, organize and write down the feedback of your strengths and weaknesses.

9. Repeat this exercise with every single person on your list.

10. There you have it, now you have a full 360 degrees of your strengths and weaknesses.

SELF-AWARENESS EXERCISE BY YOURSELF

Another way to develop self-awareness is by doing the above exercise by yourself. If you think you can be very objective and self-introspective, you can do the following exercises. Sit down and think through about all the things you are good at and all the things you may not be good at. You could also rely on online tools like CliftonStrengths and StandOut assessments as guides.

Sometimes it is more beneficial to combine both techniques. In other words, do a self-assessment as well as get help from others. Then integrate the results from both methods together to become extremely aware of your strengths and weaknesses.

In summary, knowing your strengths and weaknesses allows you to become self-aware. Self-awareness is extremely important for your career, and really gives you a sense of your assets and deficits. Self-awareness will help you determine your future career trajectory and your future jobs.

Use the self-awareness exercise on an annual basis. Over a period of time, we always evolve, develop new skills, new experiences, skill sets, and habits. Doing this exercise on an annual basis helps you keep up with yourself as you are evolving as a professional and as a human being.

KEY TAKEAWAYS

- Before you start writing down your career plan, it is important to develop self-awareness.
- Use annual exercises below to become self-aware of your skills, experiences, strengths, and weaknesses.
- Ask for honest feedback from friends, family, colleagues, or managers.
- Develop a list of strengths and weaknesses by being highly introspective and brutally honest with yourself.

RESOURCES

Being self-aware means understanding your skills, your experience, your strengths, and your weaknesses. Use tools like CliftonStrengths and StandOut assessments as guides to figure out what you're good at.

CHAPTER 10

TRIPLE DOWN ON YOUR STRENGTHS

"Your strength is your superpower."

—Rajesh Setty

"Focus on your strengths, not your weaknesses.

Focus on your character, not your reputation.

Focus on your blessings, not your misfortunes."

—Roy T. Bennett, *The Light in the Heart*

Traditional wisdom says, become self-aware, find out your strengths and weaknesses, and make sure you fix your weaknesses.

That is just plain wrong.

Successful leaders always bet on their strengths, their superpowers.

Look, don't get me wrong. If there are fundamental issues and skill gaps, they will absolutely be roadblocks for career growth. For example, you are trying to become a mobile app developer, but you don't know how to program, you're going to have a problem. Or if you are trying to become a sales leader, but you don't have basic communication skills, your sales record will be dismal. In cases like these, there are fundamental issues, which you need to fix urgently.

The real question is whether you want to devote more time to fixing your weaknesses or doubling down on your strengths.

I always give the example of Jony Ive, who was a designer at Apple and recently left the company. Jony Ive is one of the best product designers out there. His greatest strength is product design, but he might not be the best at managing people. So, he may not be equipped to run large engineering teams, but he knows his strength is industrial product design, and that's what he doubled down upon.

Once you determine your strengths and weaknesses as described in the previous chapter, you are ready to figure out how you can take the strengths that differentiate you from the rest and invest most of your energy to build on them.

How do you do that?

> Train, practice, and demonstrate
> your strengths.

You start by amplifying your strengths. Whether your strength is communication, focus, detailed analysis, or programming, or if it's a hard skill such as understanding financial information, just make sure you get better at your strength and double down on it. Actually, triple down on it.

Train more, take some external training if necessary, and practice more. Keep up this cycle until your strength becomes a muscle. This muscle memory will help you demonstrate your superpower so that people will automatically become aware that this is your strength.

Traditional wisdom might say fix your weaknesses but spending your time on your strengths will help you propel your career forward.

KEY TAKEAWAYS

- Fixing your weakness is important, but building on your strength is way more important.
- "Learn, train, practice, demonstrate" is the mantra that helps you amplify your strengths.

CHAPTER 11

T-SHAPED SKILLS FRAMEWORK

"Talent you have naturally. Skill is only developed by hours and hours and hours of beating on your craft."

—Will Smith

"All skills are perfected through the process of failure. Embrace loss as a necessary part of improvement."

—Jerry Lynch

"All skills are learnable."

—Brian Tracy

It is crucial that we learn and develop skills thoughout our careers. Let's get into some of the terminology around skills.

Skill, at the most basic level, is your ability to do certain things. Experience, on the other hand, is the time you have used that particular skill.

Let me also introduce competency in this lexicon. Competency is the combination of skills and experiences. If you have the skill of data analytics, and you have the experience of a few years of having done data analysis in particular areas or particular domains, then you have competency in data analysis.

Skills + Experience = Competency

It is quite common for people who are early in their career to have impressive skills but not enough experience, which means that they haven't quite developed the skill into a competency. So, here is my suggestion. When you have a skill, gain some experience in it, and then you have competency.

BUILD A T-SHAPED SKILL SET

Let us change our perspective a little and think from the standpoint of companies that are looking to hire top professionals. When companies think about the talent they need to hire, especially for a management or a leadership position, these companies are really looking for a T-shaped leader or a T-shaped person.

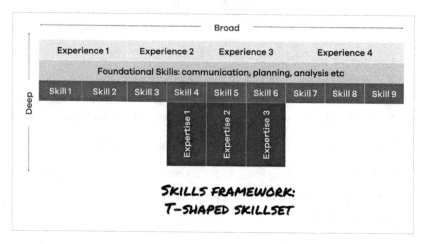

SKILLS FRAMEWORK:
T-SHAPED SKILLSET

A T-shaped leader is:

- Someone with a broad set of business and/or technology knowledge
- Combined with a deep set of expertise in particular areas

A person may have a broad set of competencies in certain business or technology areas. In addition to those competencies, they have deep expertise in specific competencies. Expertise is deep experience in a particular skill.

Expertise = Deep Experience

Your expertise allows you the opportunity to be a domain expert in specific areas. At the same time, your broad set of skills and competencies provides a broader view of the business or domain. This combination affords opportunities to engage in different areas of the business.

For example: Jen works at a tech company and has deep expertise in enterprise technology architecture. At the same time, she has enough broad skills and experience to have at least a conceptual understanding of how sales works, how supply chain works, or how HR works in her company. This skillset achieves two things for Jen: her enterprise tech architecture skills provide technical depth to give her credibility. The broad skills of understanding business operations give her the opportunity to engage with multiple stakeholders and help solve their problems. Do you think Jen is a great T-shaped person to be successful? You betcha.

In summary, T-shaped skills are a collection of your competencies: a broad set of skills combined with deep expertise. A broad set of skills is great because they form the broad part of the "T" while the narrow part of the "T" is a set of deep expertise in specific skills.

BUILD A T-SHAPED SKILLSET

Over a period of time, you can collect a broad range of business and/or technology knowledge combined with deep expertise in a particular area. Having a wide industry knowledge makes you an invaluable asset. This is not something that happens by accident. You have to actively seek out and learn more about the business and the technologies in use. Then, zero in on specific areas, identify the skills they need that match the ones you have, and develop expertise in those skills to build competencies.

Visualize what your T-shaped skills look like and think about the nature of expertise you already have. How can you leverage your expertise in a particular skill to show competency in a specific industry or vertical which will provide you with even more relevance in your current job, as well as in your future career?

What skills would you like to develop, and which of those would you like to strengthen with more expertise to develop competency? How you can further enhance these competencies to meet future market needs?

Consider the things that you may need in the future. For example, you may need design ability, analytics, a cross-cultural communication style, a global mindset, or even emotional intelligence (EQ). Think about the skills that you will need in the future. Use those ideas to build the T-shaped structure for your future skills and expertise.

KEY TAKEAWAYS

- Skill is your ability to do certain things.
- Experience is the accumulation of the years you spend honing a skill.
- Competency is skill with experience behind it.
- A T-shaped person is someone with a broad set of business and/or technology knowledge, combined with a deep set of expertise in particular skills, industries, or verticals.

CHAPTER 12

THE MARKET FRAMEWORK

"You can observe a lot by just watching."

—Yogi Berra

The market is made up of organizations that operate in different industries. Each one of these organizations has their own functions. It's really hard to figure out what the market is and where you should look for career opportunities. To plan a good and effective career strategy for yourself, it's important for you to:

- Understand what the market looks like and how it is structured.
- Figure out the areas of the market in which you really want to play.

Let's understand some market terms. The first term is an industry also known as a vertical. An industry or a vertical is a type of business, trade, or profession. For example, retail is an industry. So is healthcare. Manufacturing and life sciences are other examples.

There are different functions within each industry. Almost every company needs marketing, sales, operations, supply chain, HR, IT, and legal. There are many different functions within a company that are performed in a way that is specific to that industry, for example, the supply chain function in technology is different from that in manufacturing industries, the benefits management function in healthcare is unique, the portfolio management function in financial services is a function that is unique to that industry, etc. These are some of the unique market terms that you should aim to know about when you start to focus on an industry. Each industry has its own particular evolution, cultures, roles, and growth path.

Now look at how these industry verticals and functions interact.

Functions	Industry Verticals	Banking, and Fin Svcs	Healthcare Life Sciences	Technology, Media & Telecom	Travel, Hospitality & Aviation	Manufacturing & logistics	Energy & Utilities	Retail & Consumer Goods	Public Sector & Education	Insurance	Natural Resources
Marketing											
Sales											
Services											
Product / R&D											
Operations											
Supply Chain											
IT											
Finance											
HR, Legal etc											

MARKET FRAMEWORK

Above you'll see a table with a lot of different industries in columns: banking and financial services; healthcare and life sciences; technology, media, telecommunications, travel and hospitality; manufacturing and logistics; and energy and utilities, etc. Each company in any of these industries will need functions like marketing, sales, services, product, or research and development. They need operations, supply chain management, finance, legal, and HR. This framework helps you understand the different types of industry verticals and the functions within them.

Now, let's look at the intersection of the column of healthcare and the row of IT (a cell). This is an example of how you can identify your current place in the industry.

	Functions	Industry Verticals	Banking, and Fin Svcs	Healthcare Life Sciences	Technology, Media & Telecom	Travel, Hospitality & Aviation	Manufacturing & logistics	Energy & Utilities	Retail & Consumer Goods	Public Sector & Education	Insurance	Natural Resources
	Marketing											
Revenue enabling functions	Sales											
	Services											
	Product / R&D											
	Operations											
	Supply Chain											
Cost mgmt functions	IT											
	Finance											
	HR, Legal etc											

Diverse opportunities: culture, roles, growth and industry evolution

MARKET FRAMEWORK

The Market Framework: Diverse Career Opportunities

One important thing to understand is that some functions are revenue facing and some are cost facing. For example, marketing and sales, service, product development, and operations are revenue-facing functions, i.e., they directly influence revenue.

Then there are functions that are on the cost side of a business. Functions like supply chain operations, IT, finance, HR, and legal are examples of functions that cost the company money but enable it to function. There's no right or wrong answer in terms of the role that you want to have or the one you have today. But revenue-facing functions generally offer faster career growth and trajectory compared to cost-facing functions. There is no right or wrong answer here: it is your call where you see opportunities for yourself.

The Market Framework helps you answer a few questions to figure out what your career opportunities are:

- What is the market?
- Where are you in this market?
- Which industry and function do you belong to?

USE THE FRAMEWORK AS A CAREER RE-INVENTION TOOL

You could also use this framework as a map or as a tool for career reinvention if you're looking for a career change. This section is for folks that are looking for a transition.

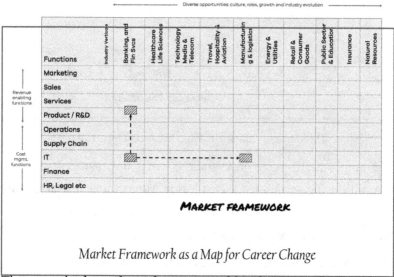

Market Framework as a Map for Career Change

The example above shows how you could make a pivot from a banking IT function to the marketing or financial service function in the same industry since you believe you have enough knowledge in the financial industry. If you understand IT well, you might want to move into the IT function of manufacturing and logistics which would be a move in the same function. This would be a one-step career change or a one-step career move.

You could also do a two-step move. This is a harder and more challenging career move. For example, you could go from doing IT in the banking industry to marketing in healthcare or life sciences industry. That's a big shift. These two-step moves require the person to be really committed to making big investments and putting in the hard work.

The Market Framework gives you a better picture of the market; a way to view the market through the lens of its verticals and functions within those verticals. You can use this to make informed decisions about your career growth and possible career moves.

If you're looking for a career change or a career reinvention, use the Market Framework to figure out which function/industry could make the best use of your skill set. The tool helps you plot where your career is now and how to get where you want your career to be.

KEY TAKEAWAYS

- Use the Market Framework to figure out which area/industry could make the best use of your skill set.
- You can also use the tool as a map to make a career move within your organization or, down the road, outside your current organization.
- This visual roadmap is helpful to clearly identify your career pathways.

RESOURCES

- The Market Framework Tool

All tools mentioned in the book can be downloaded from www.unlockthebook.com/resources

PART C

STRATEGY

"Give me six hours to chop down a tree and
I will spend the first four sharpening the axe."

—Abraham Lincoln

The **Strategy Part** is all about creating a blueprint for your career that you can reference and enhance during your leadership journey.

The Strategy Part of *Unlock!* is designed to help you clear the clutter in your mind to start the process of career transformation. This step-by-step process starts your journey with the **North Star** Step, the guide to envisioning your career plan, and takes you through a process of discovery and expansion to culminate in **Resolve Step,** where you commit to the decision you've made.

The first tool in **North Star Step** is the Envisioned Future Tool which helps visualize what your life might be like in the future. The Career Planning Tool helps you transform this information and make it more concrete. Once you write down your career plan and define how you would like to achieve your goals, your plan no longer stays a dream, but becomes an achievable objective.

The **Discovery Step** leads you through the process of uncovering your skills and competencies and defining a career stack from them. Packaging your skills and competencies in different ways helps you discover new roles and opportunities.

You learn to analyze the current and future market trends in the **Horizon Step** with the 3 Horizons Tool. Once you learn to identify the emerging trends, you become free to upskill yourself to adapt to the changing norms in the industry.

After you have written down your career plan, discovered your career stack, and expanded your horizon, you arrive at your resolve to finally make the best decision. **Resolve Step** tools not only help you identify the right decision, but also helps you commit to these career decisions.

HOW TO USE STRATEGY TOOLS MOST EFFECTIVELY

I recommend going through the set of tools in the **Strategy Part** set of tools in the following order:

- Start with the Envisioned Future and Career Planning Tools in the **North Star** Step to create a draft. Populate it to the best of your knowledge. There might be some areas you might not be able to complete. That is okay because you will be creating the content in the steps that follow this one. Creating a draft is good enough at this stage. Remember, perfection is the enemy of progress.
- Use the **Discovery Step** tools to determine your target roles. The Career Stack and Potential Roles Tools in this step will guide you.

- Move on to the **Horizon Step** to identify current and emerging market trends so that you can align your career goals with them.
- Once you've narrowed down on the goal and the roles, the Decision Making and Commitment Tools in the **Resolve Step** will help you make a decision and commit to it.

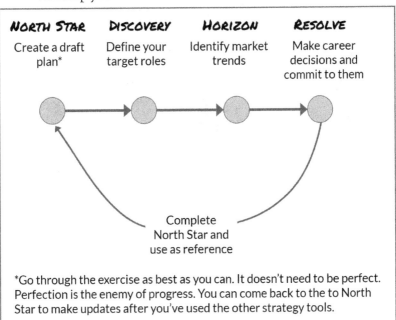

NORTH STAR	DISCOVERY	HORIZON	RESOLVE
Create a draft plan*	Define your target roles	Identify market trends	Make career decisions and commit to them

Complete
North Star and
use as reference

*Go through the exercise as best as you can. It doesn't need to be perfect. Perfection is the enemy of progress. You can come back to the to North Star to make updates after you've used the other strategy tools.

How to Use the Strategy Section

SOURCE: WWW.NAPKINSIGHTS.COM/NAPKIN/864/

CHAPTER 13

NORTH STAR: YOUR STRATEGY FOR SUCCESS

"If you don't know where you're going, any road will take you there."

—The Cheshire Cat in
Lewis Carroll's *Alice's Adventures in Wonderland*

The **North Star** Step guides you toward what you really want to do and who you would like to become.

It assists in developing a career plan to achieve your purpose. Once written, your career plan enables you to align your future actions and growth toward this **North Star**, which reduces the risk of thrashing. Thrashing happens when a person heads off in different directions that won't yield the desired outcomes. In many cases, people don't realize they are thrashing until it's too late to correct the course.

The **North Star Step** focuses your actions, activities, and energies to produce maximum results and achieve your objective.

At the same time, it is important to understand that the plan is meant to be flexible. Your plan can and should evolve as the market changes or your situation changes. The *Unlock!* career plan gives you flexibility to evolve and change it as needed.

HAVING A PLAN FOR A PLAN

Writing down a career plan is challenging. There is the daily grind. You wake up in the morning, get to work, come back in the evening, spend time with the family, have dinner, and then prepare for the next day. There isn't a lot of time during the day to sit down and write a career plan.

Here is an interesting observation. When was the last time you went on a vacation? When you did that, you planned for it, didn't you? You booked tickets in advance, figured out where you'd be going, where you'd be staying, and what activities you'd be doing. You planned what you wanted to do: go to a museum, hit the beach, or just take it easy. Whatever your goal, you spent time planning it, whether alone or with the help of someone so that everyone was aligned on the plan for your vacation. You must have spent a considerable amount of time planning it, maybe a couple of weeks or more.

Now, think about all the time you spend at work, which is the most amount of waking time you spend at any one place.

For the most part, people don't really plan their work, and they don't really plan their careers. Even though work lives span many years, people don't really spend a lot of time thinking about and planning for their careers. It might seem a bit unnatural and challenging to think strategically about the things they want to do and put together a plan.

But I guarantee you, it will be worth every single moment spent on it.

FLEXIBLE PLAN IS NOT AN OXYMORON

A career plan defines your professional goals. You may have some goals in mind, and you might have an idea of how to achieve them. You may feel there are so many external factors beyond your control that they put your plan at risk, unless you change your plan.

So, does it really make sense to have a plan?

The quick answer is, yes.

Just the act of writing down your plan will provide you a sense of direction for your work: it will fuel your actions, activities, and everything you do as part of your work. You will find new meaning in different areas of work just because you went through the exercise of writing a career plan.

A career graph is never a straight line. Every day isn't a great day. There are days when you are operating like a machine, and there are days when you're not at your 100 percent. If our careers moved in a straight line, everyone would be super successful.

But that doesn't happen. There will be problems, and there will be setbacks. But guess what? There will be more positive days than negative days. So, make sure to have a plan and learn a fundamental truth about the process. Plans can be altered. They can be updated if situations change. Your career plan does allow you that flexibility.

You can update your plan every quarter or more often, if that works for you.

Now we know it makes a lot of sense to write your own career plan. Be flexible and update the plan as needed to adjust to market changes and your unique situations.

Pro tip: As you get into writing your career plan, one quick tip is to make sure that your career plan is easily accessible. Whether it's on your laptop, you've printed it out, or it's on your phone, you need to be able to access it to review and edit it.

TO WRITE YOUR PLAN, KNOW THE FUTURE!

There are two parts to the process of writing a career plan. The first is to use Envisioned Future Tool, and the second is to develop your actual career plan.

What is an envisioned future? It's a broad, forward-looking concept in which you think with an open mind and visualize your future. The results are entered into the Envisioned Future Tool.

The information you've entered in this Envisioned Future Tool informs your use of the Career Planning Tool, which transforms vision into goals and plans to achieve them.

ENVISIONED FUTURE TOOL

The Envisioned Future Tool helps you imagine a future state where you are at your very best professionally and personally. This is a state where you are creating value for customers and stakeholders, enjoying the rewards.

Tip: Make sure to download and print the template before you start this exercise.

The tool shows a way for you to visualize a state of mind and place that you occupy at a specific time in the future. Think deeply with an open mind as you do this exercise. It is a really good way to envision your life more broadly and more futuristically. Performing this task will help you prepare for the next section on career planning.

Here's how to go about creating your envisioned future.

Pick a specific date, a specific month, and a specific year in the future. Think about the details of that day. What time of day is it? What's the weather like? Make sure to focus on details because the more specific you are, the better you visualize the day. Visualize to the point where the environment and scene feel real.

Now that you have sped up the clock, and you're in the future on a specific day, let's get into how you start using the Envisioned Future Tool. Ask yourself very specific questions:

- Where are you living?
- What is the environment like?
- Who are you with – your friends, your colleagues, your family?
- What is the type of work you're doing?
- What are the specific areas of your work?
- Who are you interacting with as part of your work?

The next section in the Envisioned Future Tool is to determine how you're helping others with the value you're creating for them. It may be value for your customers, your company, your team, your community, your organization, or even your family and friends.

- Think about the value you're providing.
- Imagine about the gifts you're giving them as part of the work that you're doing.
- Visualize how you are creating value in the market, for your customers, for your team, or for your friends and family.
- Think about the rewards you're getting.
- Imagine the fame and fortune that you will receive as part of your work.
- Think about how you're enjoying those rewards, fame, and fortune.

- Visualize how you're spending the rest of the day outside of work.
- Think about the sports that you are engaged in or the social time you are enjoying with your family.
- Think about your entire day as your envisioned future. That is the future that you are designing actively.

While you're going through this exercise, feel free to make notes. Don't forget to transfer these notes into the Envisioned Future Tool.

Pro tip: As mentioned before, the key here is to take the time to visualize; it should feel as if you are living those scenarios in the real world. This extra step will provide you the details and resolution to capture the right level of details to make this exercise work really well for you.

Pro tip: Make sure to write the vision in the present tense, as though you have accomplished it. This is intentional. By expressing them in the present tense, you are asking and activating your subconscious to move you in this direction. Powerful.

NORTH STAR: ENVISIONED FUTURE

Envisioned Future: Specific future date

- **Where are you living?**

- **Who are you with?**

- **What are you doing?** Describe the type of work you are doing

---

North Star: Envisioned Future Tool

LET'S CREATE YOUR CAREER PLAN

Writing down your career plan requires complete focus.

You will have to find a dedicated slot of about four to five hours where you can be totally by yourself. Make sure there's no one else around you so that your task receives your complete attention.

Have a good solid table in front of you and a comfortable chair in which to sit.

There must not be any distractions. Turn off your devices so that you can really focus.

Print out the Career Planning Tool templates.

Make sure you have the Envisioned Future Tool template you filled out in the earlier exercise.

Also, don't forget the notes you prepared during the mindset exercises. Take a few additional sheets of paper as well if you need to jot things down.

And finally, make sure you're caffeinated, or you have your favorite beverage by you so that you're ready to start writing your career plan.

CAREER PLANNING TOOL

It's time to jump into career planning. Career planning is all about making your envisioned future a reality. Now that you've visualized what that future looks like, let's talk about how to create your career plan and go into specific sections in the plan.

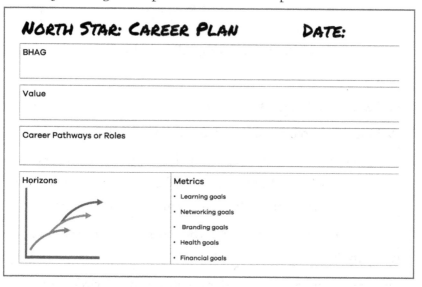

North Star: Career Plan Template

HAVE A BHAG

The first section is called BHAG, which stands for "Big, Hairy Audacious Goal." It is a concept that was first coined by Jim Collins and Jerry Poras in their 1994 book *Built to Last: Successful Habits of Visionary Companies*[10].

---

10 Collins, Jim and Jerry I. Porras, *Built to Last: Successful Habits of Visionary Companies* (HarperCollins Publishers, 2011, ISBN: 978-0060516406)

BHAG, in the context of career planning, is about setting an extraordinary goal for your career. Your BHAG must be a massive goal that spans at least few years or over a decade.

When you write down your BHAG, make sure that it is understandable and that it makes you "stretch." Remember that real growth lies outside your comfort zone. The goal must not be easy to achieve; you have to stretch yourself to fulfil it.

Make sure your BHAG is life changing. It must have a clear outcome and a clear timeline. It must be emotionally compelling enough for you to do it.

Your BHAG must represent a forward progression for you. Ideally, it shouldn't be something that you have already done in the past. For example, you might want to be a sales leader, a startup CEO, or the vice president of a particular company. Whatever your BHAG is, it must provide you with forward momentum.

One way to figure out your BHAG is to hack into it backwards. For example, think about your resume some years from now. How would you like it to read? What should be the number one line on your resume? Back plan it and your BHAG will become apparent.

Don't forget to make your BHAG exciting. If you're excited and passionate about your goal, you will do everything you can to achieve it.

For example, one of my client's BHAG was to lead a large organization (300+ people) with P&L responsibilities. Super precise. Another one's BHAG was to create a startup organization dedicated to climate change. It is clear yet ambitious.

As you see, there is no formula for BHAG. It is dependent on the future that you envision for yourself.

Important: Make sure your BHAG is a stretch goal with a clear outcome and clear timeline, and is emotionally compelling and exciting for you!

CREATE VALUE FOR OTHERS

The next section of a career plan centers around value.

As the great Zig Ziglar said, "You will get all you want in your life, if you help enough other people get what they want." If you create value for others, your actions will help you achieve your goals.

Now, "value for others" is a broad concept. Let's understand this a little bit more.

To define and capture the value you want to create for others could mean different things in different contexts. For your:

1. **Organization:** Identify internal functions, processes, technology, and people who will stand to gain from the value you create.
2. **Customers and partners:** Who will be benefiting from this value creation?
3. **Stakeholders:** Name teams and people who have a vested interest in your project or area of work.
4. **Community:** Describe a geography, a tribe, or a group of people whom you intend to serve.
5. **Family:** Yep, your goal could also be to create value for your immediate family, extended family, or your circle of friends.

These are the different entities for whom you will create value. The next set of questions are the "what" and "how" questions. What is the value you will create and how will you create it?

There are many aspects of value to consider for the "what" and "how." For example:

- Delighting your customers by creating even better products and services for them
- Helping your customers reach their goals faster and more efficiently
- Making your company's operations more effective and efficient
- Hiring, developing, and retaining talent in your company
- Helping others reach their financial goals
- Contributing and creating value in a particular community where there is limited accessibility to resources
- Giving back to your community for the unconditional support you have received
- Many others ...

You get the idea, right?

Caution: It is easy for smart people like yourself to get into what I call "solution mode," where you start getting into details of what you are going to do and how you are doing to do it. You don't need to go deep into the "what" and the "how" right now. Just having a high-level idea on your plan that shows the area where you will be creating value is good enough for now. Again, perfection is the enemy of progress. ☺

When you see the value that you will be creating for others, it will inspire you and provide the fuel for doing the things you want to do.

DEFINE YOUR NORTH STAR PATHWAYS

There may be many different paths that take you to your ultimate BHAG. The next part of your career plan is about defining your pathway.

Career progression is never a straight line. You could take a two-, three-, or even four-step process to get to your BHAG. For example, you might want to move to another domain or industry, to gain a new set of skills, transfer to a new geography, or go into a new area. It could also be a combination of all of them.

Now, with all of these things in mind, you can plan to achieve your BHAG not just by one step, but by taking a handful of steps as was discussed in the Market Framework Tool earlier. You need to figure out the different steps you need to take to achieve your BHAG. This series of steps becomes your career pathway.

ALIGN YOUR CAREER TRAJECTORY TOWARD THE MARKET

An important part of career planning is using the 3 Horizons Model Tool in the **Horizon Step** which allows you to review market trends and opportunities in order to align your career trajectory with them. You will do that when you reach that step. All the changes that happen in the market will help you accelerate your trajectory. You won't be impacted by the change but you will be leading that change.

Important: It is okay to leave this area blank for now and come back to it after you've completed that exercise.

We will be covering the **Horizon Step** in a later chapter. Please make sure you take advantage of the exercises there. Incorporate the results of the 3 Horizons Model Tool in this section of your **North Star Step** documentation.

MAKING YOUR CAREER PLAN ACTIONABLE

LEARNING PLAN SECTION: LEARNING GOALS

Always be open to having new experiences, learning new skills, and developing new competencies because continuous learning of all types is one of the foundations of your career.

Your career plan will be complete only after you have identified the skills and experience you need to achieve your goals. Skills could be hard business or technical skills: sales, digital marketing, data analysis, CRM, etc. or soft skills: emotional intelligence, communication skills, negotiation skills, etc.

You might also need experience with certain types of companies, teams, or a particular environment to reach your goal. Identify the different types of experiences and skills that you will need to achieve your goal in your career plan document.

It is okay if some of these topics are new to you. They might be areas where you have limited knowledge and experience. These new areas become part of your learning plan. While you are doing this exercise, consider all of these "gaps" as opportunities to learn.

There could be different ways to learn these skills, get experience, and address these gaps.

- Attending conferences, probably virtually in the near term
- Training in a field of your interest (see listing of apps and resources in the chapter, Market Framework)
- Taking up stretch assignments in your organization that are outside your immediate area of work
- Taking up part-time assignments or projects outside your company (make sure there is no conflict of interest!)
- Joining an interest group or meetup that is focused on a particular domain or topic (great way to build a network as well)
- In some cases, going to college to strengthen your core foundation or extend your foundation with formal education

You could select any or many of the approaches listed above to make sure that your learning goals are identified. Make sure to write down all of these learning areas in the Learning Plan section of the Career Planning Tool.

NETWORKING AND BRANDING GOALS

Networking and branding are all about telling your story.

Why is telling your story important? Because it is the best way to communicate to others the great work that you do. If you do not tell your story, then others will create a story about you. And you might not like the story that others are telling about you. ☺

That's why it is so important to have a narrative and a story (your brand) that is uniquely yours and to which others can relate. Your brand creates an environment where others feel connected to you and you are in a position to drive a much better engagement with your colleagues.

How can you best create and tell your story to others? Later on, in this book we have the **Moniker Step**, in the Brand Part, which gets into the details of how to best tell your story in person as well as online. For the purposes of this career plan document, let's identify three to five actions that you can take to develop and amplify your brand.

You can add some personal branding activities in the Networking and Branding goals section in the Career Planning tool, for example:

- Create your personal website
- Start your own blog
- Create a video series
- Write LinkedIn articles
- Speak at conferences
- Publish white papers

If for some reason, this exercise feels uncomfortable, don't worry. Write down some bullet points you think will help you with your brand. You can always come back and update this part of the Career Planning Tool after completing the **Moniker Step.**

HEALTH GOALS

All your well-designed career plans become inconsequential if your health is not on your side. Your career plan must include your health goals like maintaining a proper diet and regular exercise. Remember that your mental health is also equally important. Update the health goals portion of your career plan with activities like meditation or keeping a gratitude journal to maintain and improve your health.

FINANCIAL GOALS

There are different ways of planning your financial goals. You can have near term and intermediate goals as well as future goals.

Invest some time in planning and writing down your financial goals. Make sure you identify your top line and bottom-line goals as well. A top line is the amount of money you want to make, and a bottom line is how much you are going to save. For example, you could say that you want to have your annual compensation to be X by Y date, or you would like your savings to be $ABC or x percent of your compensation. You can even level it up by saying that your net worth needs to be at $XYZ by a certain age.

YOUR CAREER PLAN IS YOUR GUIDE

Your career plan is your guide. Keep it in a place where you can view it and review it regularly. It can be on your phone or by your desk. Performing a quarterly review at the minimum is very important to see how well you're sticking to your plan. In fact, there is a whole part of the 7 Step Process that's dedicated to tracking your career plan, and I hope you will take a look at it before you begin executing your plan.

REVIEW YOUR CAREER PLAN

Feel free to review this plan with your significant other, close friends, or colleagues whom you trust, because it is important to get their valuable input and feedback to calibrate your plan and help you correct course if need be. It is also extremely important to get their support. Your family's, colleagues', and friends' support is crucial for your growth because without it, you won't be able to hold yourself accountable.

Keep investing in your career. Never stop thinking about which skills and experiences you need to gain, and what you need to give up, so you are moving into the right areas. Sometimes you may have to eliminate planned skills and experiences that are no longer valuable for your future from your career plan in order to move forward smoothly.

KEY TAKEAWAYS

- The Envisioned Future Tool allows you to visualize your state of mind and at a specific time and place in the future. Use the template to fill in your envisioned future.
- Career planning is all about making your envisioned future a reality.
- The Career Planning Tool will provide you a sense of direction to your work.
- You can update your plan to be flexible and adaptable to any situation.
- Your Big Hairy Audacious Goal (BHAG) has to be a massive goal that you want to have in your career.
- If you create value for others, it will help you achieve your goals.
- Align your career growth toward the market so that you're leading the change.
- Learning, networking, financial, and health goals are the metrics to measure your success.

RESOURCES

- Envisioned Future Tool
- Career Planning Tool

All tools mentioned in the book can be downloaded from www.unlockthebook.com/resources

CHAPTER 14

DISCOVERY: ENDLESS POSSIBILITIES

"We all have possibilities we don't know about. We can do things we don't even dream we can do."

—Dale Carnegie

The **Discovery Step** is the process you can use to uncover new career opportunities based on your existing skills and new skills you may acquire in the future. This is a unique and exciting way to identify new roles and opportunities that might be out there for you.

The process of discovery starts with the question, "What if?"

What if you could package all your existing skills, experience, and competencies in different ways so they unlock new roles for you? These roles might be opportunities you have never considered before, and this repackaging exercise will enable you to envision yourself in new roles.

The **Discovery Step** has great tools for career reinvention if you're trying to transition into a new domain. The process will help you determine what you are capable of doing in new industries or areas.

The objective of this step is to review your skills and competencies as they exist today and make a detailed list of your top skills and expertise.

During the next step, the **Horizon Step**, you will learn to package your skills in different ways.

Be open-minded. There is no right or wrong answer here. This is a lab where you look at your skills and areas of expertise differently. So, keep an open mind and let's dive in.

MANY COMPETENCIES MAKE A CAREER STACK

The concept of discovery is based on the notion of a talent stack. Your talents are a stack of your multiple skills and experiences, or competencies.

Remember, competencies are skills plus experience. If you're skilled at something and you're experienced in that area; it is your competency.

Skills + Experience = Competency

Scott Adams, the creator of Dilbert, has shared the notion of talent stack which he defines as a list of unique skills a person might have[11]. It is a powerful concept and for the purposes of discovery, let's modify that concept a little bit to make it a "career stack." Instead of skills, let's consider competencies. As we know, skill + experience = competency.

Your career stack is a list of your competencies, the stack can have any number of competencies: three, four, five or maybe even ten.

---

11. Adams, Scott, *How to Fail at Almost Everything and Still Win Big: Kind of the Story of My Life* (Portfolio, 2014, ISBN: 978-1591847748)

WHAT DOES THE CAREER STACK MEAN FOR YOU?

The top 1 percent of professionals are the most successful. They get paid the most and they are most in demand. However, it's very hard to be among the top 1 percent of any profession. So how do you get over this dilemma?

Before discussing the solution, let's broaden that out a little bit more. Let's go from a top 1 percent to maybe the top 25 percent since that is a relatively easy target. This is about one in four people. The first attainable target you can set for yourself can be to become a professional in the top 25 percent for a particular business or technology domain area.

What are the handful of competencies that place you in the top 25 percent, i.e. higher than 3 people that you know in this area?

Consider at least four or five areas. Once you have this list, combine multiple competencies from the list in unique ways, and you can figure out how to be extraordinarily successful in certain types of roles.

PACKAGING YOURSELF: FROM GOOD SKILLS TO GREAT ROLES

This step requires you to identify those competencies at which you excel, and then figure out how to define your unique packaging. These competencies may seem basic, but if you package them in a certain way, they become extraordinary.

Here are some examples of using unique career stacks.

Example 1: If you have the following unique competencies ...

- Marketing
- Presentations

- Numbers, or analytics
- Social media

... then you could be a digital marketing leader with this stack.

Example 2: If you have the following unique competencies ...

- Technical knowledge of IT systems
- Communication
- Leadership
- Influence

... then you could be a tech architect with this stack.

In other words, your career stack requires you to define unique combinations of the competencies at which you're really good to create a new role for yourself.

DISCOVERY TOOLS

How do you become aware of your competencies? Go back to the self-awareness exercise discussed in chapter nine, "Do You Know Who You Are?"

Using the self-awareness tools discussed in that chapter, you can identify your skills and areas of experience to figure out your competencies. You can request input from a friend, a colleague, or a manager to get more insights into your skills and expertise.

Start with a list of your competencies. It is recommended that you identify between four to eight different competencies to make this exercise work.

DISCOVERY: CAREER STACK TOOL

Competency 1	Competency 6
Competency 2	Competency 7
Competency 3	Competency 8
Competency 4	New competency 1
Competency 5	New competency 2

In the Career Stack Tool, you will see that there are ten boxes for you to fill in with your competencies. Eight of these are for the existing competencies you've identified and two are for the competencies you will learn in the future. If you listed some in the learning goals section of your Career Planning Tool, use them.

In the New Roles Tool, there are five boxes in which you can fill in up to five competencies. Once you finish this exercise, you can fill in a new role / title and description.

```
DISCOVERY: NEW ROLES TOOL

                                      New role title
┌────────────────────────────┐      ┌──────────────────────────┐
│ Competency                 │      │                          │
└────────────────────────────┘      └──────────────────────────┘

┌────────────────────────────┐       New role description
│ Competency                 │      ┌──────────────────────────┐
└────────────────────────────┘      │                          │
                              ==     │                          │
┌────────────────────────────┐      │                          │
│ Competency                 │      │                          │
└────────────────────────────┘      │                          │
                                     │                          │
┌────────────────────────────┐      │                          │
│ Competency                 │      │                          │
└────────────────────────────┘      └──────────────────────────┘

┌────────────────────────────┐
│ Competency                 │
└────────────────────────────┘
```

With this intro, let's dive into using the **Discovery Step** Tools.

DIVE INTO THE DISCOVERY TOOLS

Here are the steps to follow to use these tools:

- Write down a minimum of four and a maximum of ten competencies in the boxes provided in the Career Stack Tool.
- Once you write down competencies, think about unique combinations for each one of these. While one combination could be the competencies in boxes 1, 4, 7, and 8, another combination could be 2, 3, 6, and 9.
- As you explore these unique combinations, you will come across a combination that starts to make sense to you.
- When you come up with a unique combination, imagine what an ideal role for this combination could be? What would this role with these unique competencies do?

- Come up with some additional details for that role. Any additional information or details for this role are helpful. Examples would be size of the company, industry, geography, etc.

- Once you come up with ideas of roles for a unique combination, turn to the Potential Roles Tool to document this new role.

- A quick word of **caution**: It is important for a smart person like yourself to not overthink this ☺ It is easy to fall into the trap asking questions like "Is this a real role?" or "How can I possibly do this role?" etc. Remember, the intent of this exercise is not to judge these roles but brainstorm ideas for new roles based on your competencies. The additional analysis and judgment part will come a bit later in this process when we get into feedback.

- Now you can go back to the Career Stack Tool to identify some more roles.

- Go through this exercise again and identify three to five new roles. You might need to print the template sheet multiple times for this exercise.

- **Pro tip**: Use the new competency sections to identify even more roles. New competencies are those you wish to achieve based on new market trends. Use these new competencies to imagine new types of roles. This is a great hack to identify roles you will be aiming for in the future.

- Feedback: Once you've gone through this exercise, you can share these roles with a trusted friend or colleague and get their feedback. Feedback with your trusted connections helps you to:

- Get a reality check: how can this role be possible for you?
- Identify other possible competency combinations and roles or suggest new competencies you can build. You can then add these competencies to your learning goals and design a plan to acquire them.

Pro tip: View these new roles through the **Ikigai lens**. Refer to chapter six in the Preparation Part to see how the roles you've designated align with the four circles of Ikigai. If you need more data for this work, don't worry. The **Horizon Step** and **Resolve Step** will help you refine your decisions.

The tools in the **Discovery Step** are fun exercises to use to identify your competencies, skills, and experiences in different ways so you can figure out the possibilities that exist for you out there.

KEY TAKEAWAYS

ANSWER THE "WHAT IF?"

The Discovery Step allows you to take a step back and analyze just what you're good at and how competent you are at it. Once you recognize your competencies, repackage them and identify four or five roles for yourself. The tools are ideal to detect new roles and career opportunities based on existing skills and new skills you may acquire in the future.

- Your career stack is a list of your competencies. The number of competencies on your career stack can be three, four, five, or maybe even ten.
- Seemingly ordinary skills, if you package them in a certain way, become extraordinary.
- The Discovery Step toolset is ideal to discover new roles and career opportunities based on existing skills and any new skills you may acquire in the future.
- Make a list of these roles as your target roles for future career paths.

RESOURCES

- Career Stack Tool
- New Roles Tool

All tools mentioned in the book can be downloaded from www.unlockthebook.com/resources

CHAPTER 15

HORIZON: CAPTURE MARKET TRENDS

"The price of ability does not depend on merit but on supply and demand."

—George Bernard Shaw

We often ask this question of ourselves: "Where should I take my career next?" We are always looking for something or someone who can provide us the answer. The 3 Horizons Tool is designed to answer this very question. It is based on the 3 Horizon Model.

The 3 Horizon Model[12] is a classic management framework for growth. It is used by companies all over the world and provides a structure to review your current as well as future opportunities for growth without sacrificing your current performance. The 3 Horizon Model takes the risk out of planning for the future.

The 3 Horizons Tool can be used to assess the current market trends as well as the emerging and future ones. This will guide you to align

---

12. Steve Coley, *Enduring Ideas: "The Three Horizons of Growth,"* McKinsey Quarterly, December 2009, https://www.mckinsey.com/business-functions/strategy-and-corporate-finance/our-insights/enduring-ideas-the-three-horizons-of-growth

your career trajectory by taking advantage of trends. Instead of being impacted or blindsided by these market changes, you lead those changes.

Using the 3 Horizons Tool and its associated tool provides an effective approach toward identifying market opportunities.

You've already gone through an exercise in the Preparation Part where you did research on market trends. Have the notes from the work you've already done during that part: market trends, as well as the work you've done on self-awareness.

The 3 Horizons Tool helps identify not only what's happening today but also what's emerging and on the cutting edge from business and technology perspectives.

There are three horizons in the 3 Horizons Tool. I know, surprise, surprise.

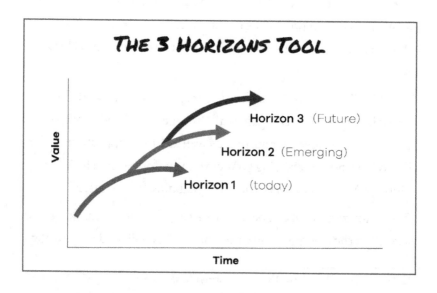

HORIZON 1: IN THE NOW AND PRESENT

Horizon 1 is about the intersection of current market needs and your current competencies. Horizon 1 indicates your current job or career domain where you are gainfully employed and creating value in a certain industry and function. You're operating in a specific zone and making a certain amount of compensation. The job you have now is your bread and butter for today. There are well-defined trends and areas in your industry/market, and your work is within those areas. So, your skills and experience, your overall competencies, are likely well aligned to the current market needs. Your compensation is a function of the value that you're bringing to the market.

HORIZON 2: IN THE NEAR FUTURE

Horizon 2 is designed to look at emerging or intermediate market needs. Once you have identified them, you can make a plan to upgrade some of your existing competencies and develop some new ones to be prepared for these emerging market needs.

One question I'm often asked is, "What do you mean by intermediate?" Intermediate could mean different things for different people, and it depends on the industry that you're in.

If you are in the tech space, it could be a shorter timeline. It could be anywhere from six months to the next couple of years; market changes or disruptions can happen in a one year to three-year cycle. Disruptions are business or technology changes that interrupt the status quo and bring a transformative change in a particular industry or multiple industries.

Accounting for disruption: We need to watch out for any business or technology disruption. By identifying the direction of business or technology changes, we can stay relevant in our domain and create value for customers, stakeholders, and our teams.

If you're in an industry where innovation cycles are longer, like healthcare or manufacturing, your intermediate cycle could be a three-year to five-year cycle, or even longer.

HORIZON 3: OVER THE LONG TERM

The last horizon in the tool is Horizon 3. Horizon 3 is where you identify entirely new market needs that need new competencies – new skills and experiences that you might not have today. These market needs are typically areas of brand new, cutting-edge technologies and businesses. Horizon 3 is also a space to explore high risk and high reward because these market needs will occur in the long-term future which is hard to predict. These market changes might occur during the next three to five years, or even longer.

To summarize, Horizon 1 is for today, Horizon 2 is for intermediate time, and Horizon 3 is for long-term future planning.

Now let's look at how to use the 3 Horizons Tool.

USING THE 3 HORIZONS TOOL

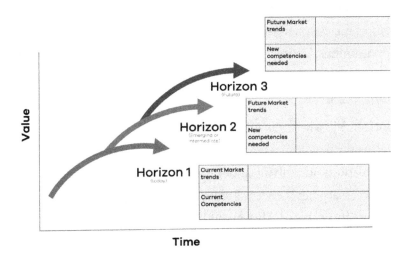

THE 3 HORIZONS TOOL TEMPLATE

In the Horizon 1 box, write down where you are currently working and what kind of role or job you are in. Describe how you're applying your skills and experience to that area. This section, when finished, gives you a good idea of your current role.

Before filling in Horizon 2, you will need to do some research around market trends and needs.

There are multiple ways to identify them:

- **Read:** Review the leading blogs and websites for your industry and adjacent industries to familiarize yourself with current and future trends.
- **Ask:** Identify people in your network who are "in the know." Ask them for an in-person meeting or phone conversation to

get their view on future market needs. Talk to friends, colleagues, and managers to understand what trends are emerging in your industry and other adjacent industries. Once you have completed this research, list the intermediate trends for the next one to three years in the Horizon 2 box. Determine the competencies you must possess to take advantage of those market opportunities. Write these competencies in the box, noting which ones you have now and which you must obtain. That completes your Horizon 2 area.

Horizon 3 is where you identify new markets and market needs, as well as the new competencies that you will need to compete in these new markets. Identifying and learning new skills as well as gaining the necessary experience is a small investment on your part to invest in those future trends that might have a massive payoff.

There are multiple ways to understanding market trends in your industry.

- **Your network:** Contact trusted experts in your network who will likely have an ear to the ground in terms of market insights. The first step is to tap into those who are directly related to the areas you are interested to explore. After exhausting the first step, if you need more information, the next step would be to get in touch with folks who might be somewhat related to your target areas. I've found that sometimes experts who are seemingly unrelated to certain domains, do have unique insights from their vantage point.
- **Online content:** Probably the easiest way to research would be to Google for information, but at the same time, you might be looking for needles in a haystack because there is so much content noise out there. One quick tip is to include "type:" in

Google searches. For example, if you add "type: PDF" in your search, you will get all PDF results. This approach can help you get to real meaty content vs noise. Also, I'd highly recommend searching podcasts, LinkedIn, and industry-specific portals like TechCrunch to get a robust selection.

- **Books:** To get deeper into specific topics, books are your best bet. Whether you make a quick trip to the library or buy one online, this is your vehicle to get deeper into market trends. Just make sure the book is recent or at least the latest edition.

- **Periodicals and magazines:** These resources will give you the most recent information. Most of the magazines carry interviews with industry leaders which help to get different perspectives. Many of these periodicals are now moving to online content so you might be better off going to the websites of these magazines for better navigation.

- **Analyst reports:** If you can get a hold of recent analyst reports from leading analyst firms, these will give you a pretty good sense of industry direction.

You don't need to put all your eggs in the same basket. Put most of your eggs in the current market needs (Horizon 1) and some of them in the emerging areas (Horizon 2). You should also put a few of them in cutting-edge technologies or businesses (Horizon 3) because they could have a big payoff if certain businesses or certain types of technologies take off. That's where you will find the biggest bang for your buck, but it is less predictable.

Pro tip: As you discover Horizon 2 and Horizon 3 areas, it is quite likely you might need additional competencies (skills and experience) to take advantage of these trends for career growth. Make sure to add these net new competencies to the Learning Goals section in your Career Planning Tool. That's how you ensure that these new skills are on your radar to learn and master.

Now let's look at an example of using the 3 Horizons Tool.

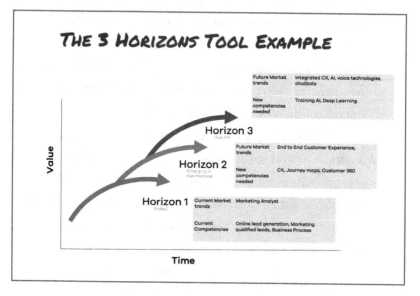

Imagine that Bob's current role is as a marketing analyst in a tech company. As a marketing analyst, he is working on online lead generation and developing qualified leads. Bob reviews his current area of work and documents and inputs this information in the Horizon 1 box of the 3 Horizons Tool. This role is where he is currently creating value, and it becomes his starting point.

Next, Bob has set up some time with his former manager, Sally, at Next Gen, Inc. Sally is an expert in the tech marketing area, and Bob trusts her judgement. Over a video conference call, Sally and Bob catch up. She shares with Bob a preview of potential tech marketing trends that will likely happen in the next couple of years. One of the important trends is improvements in customer experience. Creating an end-to-end customer experience is going to be a crucial factor for tech and almost all other industries. Bob is delighted to have found this trend that he can use for the 3 Horizons Tool exercise.

As he documents the improved customer experience trend in the Horizon 2 box, he realizes he might need additional skills to take advantage of this trend. Using his Career Stack Tool, part of the **Discovery Step**, Bob identifies the specific competencies (skills and experience) that will be required for customer experience. He goes back to the Career Planning Tool and adds these new skills to the Learning Goals section. This way, he makes sure that these new skills are part of the plan and on his radar to master.

Bob works additional market research using a collection of analyst websites and blogs to understand the potential market trends in the next five years and how things might shape up in his industry. He finds that multiple reports are indicating that integrated customer experiences, artificial intelligence, voice technologies, and chatbots are going to be the waves of the future. Bob diligently notes down those areas in the Horizon 3 box. He also notes the potential skills he will need to develop in the Learning Goals section of the Career Planning Tool.

As he wraps up the 3 Horizons Tool work, he sees that he now has a clear roadmap of what is happening today, where he is at, and what are the things he needs to focus on for the future. This also gives an idea as to where he needs to build new competencies to take advantage of future market trends.

Pro tip: It is also recommended that you discuss the results of the 3 Horizons Tool work with your trusted network and mentors. You will get invaluable insights from them as you sip caffeinated beverages while discussing the results of using the 3 Horizons Tool.

There you have it. You have completed the 3 Horizons Tool and you have identified competencies which will help you today as well as in the future. This is also an important time for you to integrate all these future competencies into the Learning Goals section of the Career Planning Tool. This will help you capitalize on all the research you've done. Once your competencies are integrated into your Career Planning Tool, you make a commitment to achieve them. Soon you will have these skills and experience under your belt.

KEY TAKEAWAYS

- The 3 Horizon Model is a classic management framework for growth. It provides a structure to review your current opportunities as well as future opportunities for growth without sacrificing your current performance.
- Horizon 1 defines current market needs and maps your current competencies to those to ensure they are aligned.
- Horizon 2 identifies emerging market needs. The career planner determines which of their existing competencies need an upgrade and determines new ones needed to take care of emerging market needs.
- Horizon 3 detects entirely new, long-term market needs, which might result from the creation of new markets or technology. These are typically areas of brand-new, cutting-edge technologies and businesses. If you don't have the skills to be competitive, add these missing elements to the learning section of your Career Planning Tool.

RESOURCES

- 3 Horizon Model

All tools mentioned in the book can be downloaded from www.unlockthebook.com/resources

CHAPTER 16

RESOLVE: MAKE BOLD CAREER DECISIONS

"Hard choices, easy life. Easy choices, hard life."

—Jerzy Gregorek

By now, you have identified a set of new roles and opportunities using the **Discovery Step**. You have also identified an industry area or domain area that will be in demand in the future using the 3 Horizons Tool. You have gone back to the **North Star** documentation and made updates to the Career Planning Tool based on things that you have learned in the **Discovery Step** and the **Horizon Step**; you have created an excellent career strategy for yourself in the **North Star** Step.

But are you ready to make a decision? Are you ready to make a commitment? That's where the **Resolve Step** comes in.

The **Resolve Step** is about making decisions based on all the facts that you can gather and committing to these decisions professionally and emotionally.

Leadership is about action. After thoughtful analysis, we've created a career strategy. It's time to commit and bring the strategy to life.

I really like the quote, "Hard choices, easy life. Easy choices, hard life." When we make a few hard choices or take tough decisions and then commit to them, our life becomes simplified and clear. Whereas when we make easy choices and fail to go through all the facets of the decision-making process, we face a harder life because we are making ongoing trade-offs and choices.

In this chapter, I'm going to help you figure out how to make tough decisions and commit to them.

100 PERCENT COMMITMENT VERSUS 95 PERCENT COMMITMENT

It might seem counter-intuitive but making a 100 percent commitment to a decision is easier than making a 95 percent commitment. Jack Canfield, author of *The Success Principles*, says "Successful people adhere to the 'no exceptions rule' when it comes to their daily disciplines[13]. Once you make a 100-percent commitment to something, there are no exceptions." It is managing these exceptions that drain us mentally and physically.

Committing 100 percent is easier than committing 95 percent because then there are no exceptions to remember and no ongoing decisions to make. Life becomes clear and simple.

Let's get into decision-making. You make decisions every day. They can be small decisions like where you want to go for lunch. They can be large decisions, which impact your life over a long period of time, like whether you should accept a job offer, relocate for better career

---

13. Canfield, Jack, *The Success Principles: How to Get from Where You Are to Where You Want to Be* (William Morrow Paperbacks, 2006, ISBN: 978-0060594893)

prospects, or change your career trajectory toward a new domain area. It is crucial for you to pause and think before making these decisions. Decision-making can be hard. You have to ensure you have approached the problem from every single angle, though sometimes, we tend to over-analyze and drive ourselves to the analysis paralysis mode where we always analyze and never commit.

Let's walk through how you can make a career decision and commit to it. Let's approach it as two separate tools – first, using the Decision Making Tool and second, the Commitment Tool.

OWN IT! USING THE DECISION MAKING TOOL

The Decision Making Tool helps us to make critical decisions as we review all the options that are in front of us. Here's an example. Let's say you have three options in front of you, and you want to get as many facts and data as you can about those options. Consider not only the upside but also any downside that might be associated with each potential decision. Look at the variable data points from different angles – professional, financial, health, family, wellness, and any other factor that comes to mind. Once you've gathered these facts, you'll be in a position to stare and compare. This analysis empowers you to own the decision-making process and make the best decision for yourself based on all the data points.

You can share the results of the process with your partner, family, and close friends for their feedback and input that might indicate the correctness of the decision that you have made.

RESOLVE: DECISION MAKING TOOL

Resolve: Decision Making Tool

Decision   Which role should I take?

		Option 1 Product Leader	Option 2 Sales	Option 3 Customer Success
Career	Pros + + Cons –			
Financial	Pros + + Cons –			
Family	Pros + + Cons –			
Health	Pros + + Cons –			
Mental / emotional	Pros + + Cons –			

Let's walk through this tool. This tool contains three options and five categories of information.

You can use this tool to make decisions between two or more options. In this scenario, we will see how to make a decision between different career options.

The first step is to transfer three of your possible target roles/industries from the Potential Roles Tool in the **Discovery Step** to the Decision Making Tool's top three column headings. Then for each role/industry (option), investigate the following aspects using the intersection of the relevant row and column. Let's call that intersection a "bucket."

As we get into this walk through, remember: we are comparing two or more options to make the best-informed decision possible.

Career: This row of the tool allows you to identify the career-related pros and cons of implementing a proposed option on your career trajectory, your continuum of jobs, and your functional domain. The intent is to figure out the impact of this option on your career: both the positive and negative impacts.

Financial: This row is for the financial impacts of your options, both positive and/or negative.

Family: This row allows you to define the impact the option might have on your family. There will be pros and cons which you will have to give a lot of consideration.

Health: Here you need to approach your options from a physical health perspective as well. This is extremely crucial. For example, ask yourself, "How much time will be spent commuting? Will I get enough time to exercise during the day or the week?" Input your answers on this row.

Mental and emotional: Ask yourself, "Will this option complement my mental health? Will my emotional wellbeing be okay going for this option?"

THE DECISION-MAKING PROCESS

So how do you use this tool?

First, name the three options you've chosen from the Potential Roles Tool from the **Discovery Step.** You can call them Career Option One or Career Path One or Job One. Each row will have the five categories in which to identify the pros and cons for each option.

Career Bucket: Let's look at an example of the career row for the first option. Imagine you're trying to develop a career in the analytics domain. The pro could be that you can make a big mark here because you have an analytical set of skills. The con could be that you don't have a big network in this space, and you will need to build that network, which means putting in a lot of effort. The pros and cons go into the career bucket: the intersection of the career row and Option 1 or Option 2 or Option 3.

Let's look at the career bucket for option two. On the plus side, option two might be a strategic move for your career, and you are passionate about it. The downside is a lower title, or a title that you don't want.

Make sure for each option, you have a pro and a con for each bucket.

Other Buckets: Let's walk through the rest of the buckets. The second bucket is financial. The pro for the first job option could be better compensation, benefits, 401(k), or retirement plans. The con could be the opposite.

When it comes to family, you must ask yourself these questions. Does your option give you more family time? Is it aligned with the strategic interests of your family? Remember to write down all the pros and cons you can think of.

In your physical health bucket for each job, you have to ensure the option still gives you the ability to maintain your physical health. Will the option give you a long commute or a short commute? How will that affect your health? How often will you get physical exercise? Will too much stress in the job cause you to overeat?

The mental and emotional category is about managing stress and mental health. How much stress will you be expected to handle? Are there opportunities for you to maintain and manage your mental health? This bucket for each option is crucial; you have to make sure that you're comparing all the options across the mental and emotional health row.

Decisions are deeply personal, so the importance of each row will not be uniform for everyone. For example, you might feel that your career is the most important aspect, and you want to prioritize that over everything else. Or you might feel that your family comes first and want to prioritize them. For some, your health might require more attention. So, that will be the first row to focus on. For others, financial stability might drive your decisions.

Whatever your priority row is, add as much relevant data as you can to each bucket. Remember, the more data you put in, the more you'll get out of the tool. Once you have a completed sheet in your hand, sit down, pick up your coffee, tea, or favorite beverage, and take a good, hard look at it. Do a stare-and-compare between the three options and arrive at the right decision for you.

Review the information you have entered with your significant other, family, close friends, and anyone else who has a stake in your career decisions. Listen carefully to their feedback and potential suggestions.

This tool provides a very objective and an unemotional approach to making a great decision with all the relevant facts laid out in front of you.

Now that you have made a decision – assuming you like the decision – let's look at what's holding you back.

What is keeping you from turning your decision into reality?

How can you execute your decision?

How can you commit the time, resources, and the emotional strength that you need to enact this decision?

RESOLVE: COMMITMENT TOOL

Professional	Personal
Examples • Skills • Education • Network • Geography • Manager / Stakeholders • Others?	Examples • Family • Social • Emotional • Mindset • Others?

The Commitment Tool is divided into two columns. The first column is for your objections, all the things that are holding you back from executing your decision. This tool is left blank by design because you will need to go freeform on this one. Just start writing. Write with no inhibitions. You don't have to think about the solutions yet. The objections can be professional, emotional, physical, financial, or any other aspect of the decision that concerns you.

Your objections could be professional. You might feel that you don't have the right skills, the right education or pedigree, or the right network. For example, "I have a great fear of public speaking and this job will require a lot it".

They could also be personal. You might feel that you don't have the right professional or emotional mindset to do a particular kind of work.

Here's the beautiful part. This list can be as long as you want.

Now, go to the second column. Assess the first objection you have written down in the first column. Ask yourself whether the objection is valid. If it is valid, then is it a solvable problem? Write down the solution in the second column.

Repeat the process for each objection.

I *guarantee* you each of these objections are solvable. Often, we come up with these objections and excuses to stop ourselves from enacting big decisions. It might sound strange, but you are your own worst enemy. The Commitment Tool helps you overcome these objections. Sometimes, the solution is right in front of you. All you might have to do is make a few changes in your environment or yourself to remove the objection.

Now that you have found solutions to things that have been holding you back, there's nothing that can stop you from committing to your decision and moving forward.

As you move forward by committing to your decision with the Commitment Tool, you're not only going in a great direction, but now, you have more wood behind the arrow. You have rationale. You've fixed the things that were preventing you from moving forward. You can go out there, execute your decision, and take actions to make an amazing career trajectory happen.

KEY TAKEAWAYS

- The Decision Making Tool simplifies the decision-making process by enabling you to break down your options and arrive at the best decision for you.
- There are five buckets for each role option in this tool: career, financial, family, physical health and emotional/mental health. By asking questions relevant to each category, you can ensure that the decision you are about to make is completely thought through and you are comfortable with it.
- The Commitment Tool enables you to execute your decision while giving you a free hand in choosing it.

RESOURCES

- Decision Making Tool
- Commitment Tool

All tools mentioned in the book can be downloaded from www.unlockthebook.com/resources

PART D

YOUR PERSONAL BRAND

Your personal brand is the story of who you are and what you can do. It gives you your true label, which defines others' expectations of you.

Who is in charge of building your brand? Who is responsible for telling your story? Who decides what your capabilities are?

It is You.

Building your personal brand is more about having a strategy rather than leaving it to serendipity. You need to have a structured plan to develop your brand and tell your story, and more importantly, maintaining it. This is how you build credibility. Effectively showcasing your work through a polished online brand opens up avenues of growth and development.

YOU CAN RARELY
BUILD A POWERFUL
IDENTITY BY JUST
WISHING FOR ONE!
X WISHFUL THINKING
✓ WORK

SOURCE: WWW.NAPKINSIGHTS.COM/NAPKIN/861/

CHAPTER 17

MONIKER: DEFINE YOUR PERSONAL BRAND

"Your brand is what other people say about you when you're not in the room."

—Jeff Bezos

Your company has a brand. Your company's products and services have a brand. Similarly, you have a brand too. It is a personal brand. Your personal brand is about your story, what you stand for and what you are known for. It is reflected in how people around you engage with you, work with you, and make requests of you.

Your brand and your story create a certain expectation of you. Cultivating and building a great personal brand happens over a period of time.

But it does require a conscious effort to build your personal brand.

If you do not tell your story, it creates an "absence of narrative." An absence of narrative creates a vacuum about who you are and what you stand for. In this vacuum, others will manufacture a narrative to describe you, because they do not know enough about you. You may not like what they come up with. It makes much more sense to create your narrative, share your story, and provide that storyline for others to learn about you.

YOUR PERSONAL BRAND

A brand is people's opinion about you. It's their perception of you. As Jeff Bezos says, "It's what people say about you when you're not in the room."

Having an online personal brand is extremely important because you never know when people will look you up online. People do look you up online all the time. In fact, most people will search for you online before they have a meeting with you. Before any exchange of emails happens, your stakeholders or customers have most likely checked your online "brand." Creating and maintaining your online brand becomes crucial since it will help you tell the right story when people look for you. If the online story and in-person story are not aligned, you might lose credibility. Another quick way to lose credibility is to have a "zero online brand." It is as if you do not exist or you might be mistaken for a charlatan.

Developing your narrative and story is the way to create an online and personal brand. Whether you are introducing yourself in a meeting or over email, you are sharing your narrative and story. And, you should be able to tell it confidently and convincingly.

Think about yourself as a company.

If you visualize yourself as You Inc, then a new set of possibilities emerge: you have a brand, you have a product, you have a story to tell.

> All your skills, talents, and experience could end up being useless if you lack a polished online brand.

BODY OF WORK STRATEGY

Now that we've talked about the why, let's talk about the what and the how of personal branding.

One technique to create a great online brand is the Body of Work Strategy. This technique helps you create artifacts and content that enable you to showcase your work and demonstrate your expertise.

Pamela Slim, the award-winning author of *Body of Work*[14], shares this insight, "Focusing on building a body of work will give you more freedom and clarity to choose different work options throughout the course of your life, and you'll be able to connect your diverse accomplishments, sell your story, and continually reinvent and relaunch your brand."

How do you do that?

- First, make sure you have gone through the Preparation Part, as well as the **North Star**, **Discovery**, and **Horizon Steps** to identify strengths, current roles, and potential future roles.
- Make a list of all the online properties where you have a presence. LinkedIn, Facebook, Instagram, Medium, and your blog are all examples of online properties.
- The next step is to make sure that the content you have across

---

14. Slim, Pamela, *Body of Works: Finding the Thread That Ties Your Story Together* (Portfolio, 2013, ISBN: 978-1591846192)

all these properties reflects your personal brand and body of work. This content should be reflective of your unique perspectives, your concepts, and your ideas.

When you create a video or an online presentation, or if you're posting pictures of yourself doing something exciting in an area where there's high demand, it's extremely likely that people will gravitate toward you. This means that people will start engaging and connecting with you in more ways than you could imagine.

In the age of hyper-connectedness, you should create a body of work about yourself, leveraging all the online properties at your disposal and making sure that they are telling a coherent story. That's what creating an online brand is all about.

HUB & SPOKE: IMPLEMENTING THE BODY OF WORK STRATEGY

To curate a coherent online story that communicates your identity, you can use what I call the Hub & Spoke Strategy.

Hub & Spoke Strategy

At the center is your hub, your primary domain. It could be your FirstNameLastName.com; it could be your blog; it could be whatever you think your domain should be. This is your permanent place on the internet. This is your hub. People should be able to come to xyz.com and be able to connect with you.

From this primary domain, we have the spokes that connect to this hub, such as LinkedIn, Facebook, SlideShare, Instagram, YouTube, and blogs.

Of these, LinkedIn is the preferred tool of professionals.

A personal favorite of mine is SlideShare. SlideShare allows you to post presentations to make really strong arguments and display thought leadership. It's easy to get started on SlideShare, and you can repurpose content from your blog, for example, to highlight your opinions.

If you're not using all the spokes in the wheel, your online brand is not running at optimum speed.

By leveraging the power of the Hub & Spoke Strategy, you can craft a unique, consistent, online brand from which others can engage with you about your ideas, experiences, and concepts.

Investing in the Hub & Spoke Strategy has a compounding effect. Over time, as you keep building your online presence, people will be able to connect more with your online brand.

Now that we've seen how to create a personal brand, let's improve how we show up in person: physically or more important, virtually as well.

CHANGE THE GAME: ELEVATOR PITCH

A lot of people introduce themselves too casually. "Hi, I'm Kyle and I work at company X."

A basic introduction doesn't provide many avenues for engagement. It doesn't provide a flow or a narrative. It doesn't give others an opportunity to engage. The best response you can get for such an introduction is, "Okay."

And that's not a great response.

The elevator pitch helps you present yourself in the best light possible. It helps you differentiate yourself from others and sets you up for more engagement. When you give your elevator pitch, there should be a curiosity angle. People should ask you, "Oh, that's interesting. Tell me more." That then becomes an interesting angle for you to use to continue the conversation.

Learning to give an elevator pitch is very important because it's a tool to have a conversation and engage with others.

CREATE AND DELIVER THE PERFECT ELEVATOR PITCH

There are five components to constructing your elevator pitch.

1. WHO AM I?

Introduce yourself. You can say, "Hey, I'm Kyle. I'm the manager of XYZ." The title is optional. If you want to leave your title out of it, that's fine too.

2. WHAT BUSINESS AM I IN?

Explain your business, your domain, or the work that you do. You can mention your company or your industry. For example, you can say, "Hey, I'm Kyle, I'm in financial services." Here financial services is your domain.

3. WHAT GROUP OF PEOPLE DO I SERVE?

One of the most important pieces of the elevator pitch lays out who gets the benefit of your work. Let people know who gets the advantage of working with you and who gets value by working with you. Define who your customers and your stakeholders are.

"Hey, I'm Kyle. I provide financial services to people of high net worth."

4. WHAT IS MY SPECIALTY OR MY UNIQUE SELLING PROPOSITION (USP)?

The USP is an interesting aspect of the pitch where you can highlight the special skills you bring to the table and some unique areas of value that you create. You can talk about your competency or your unique abilities to do certain things that no one else can and differentiate yourself from others. Be sure to bring out your unique perspectives during this phase of your pitch.

5. WHAT BENEFITS DO YOUR STAKEHOLDERS GET FROM YOUR WORK?

Share the results and specific data points with others. For example,

Example 1: "Hey, I'm Jenny. I'm a sales expert for SaaS companies. I've been able to create unique value for customers by creating sales acceleration tools."

Example 2: "Hi, I'm Kyle. I provide financial service for high net worth individuals. My specialty is that I provide an accelerated path to wealth creation and retirement!"

There are so many other examples where you can weave these five components into your everyday language and start to create a very different introduction for yourself.

To summarize, in an elevator pitch, talk about:

- Who you are (summary)
- The business you're in or the area of work you're in
- Your customers or your stakeholders
- Your USP
- The benefits others get from you, including tangible elements that you create for others and how you deliver results for them

Once you have these five things down, start to practice. Practicing is one of the most important things about an elevator pitch. Practice your elevator pitch in front of a mirror, or even better, record yourself. When you record yourself, you can observe how you talk and how you're delivering the pitch. This will help you identify points you may want to tweak and help you correct your course so that your delivery is better. More often than not, it's all about the delivery.

> Content is important, but the delivery is what drives the point home.

Lastly, your elevator pitch should flow naturally, and it shouldn't feel like it's rehearsed. The more natural you are about it, the better the delivery. Once you have a solid elevator pitch, you'll be able to introduce yourself well at your next meeting, webinar, or networking event.

HERE IS HOW TO PITCH!

Now that we've seen how to create an elevator pitch, let's discuss how to use it. First, here are a few instances in which you can use your elevator pitch.

Use your elevator pitch to introduce yourself in meetings, conferences, networking events, or even in your interviews. Put yourself in a good light and in a very clearly differentiated way.

Use your elevator pitch, or some form of it, as a way to do email introductions. This is a really clear way for you to introduce yourself over email to a new person or even over LinkedIn.

You can also put the pitch on your LinkedIn profile. Your LinkedIn profile is a place you really want to differentiate yourself. Your elevator pitch helps you do this. It can add a lot of value to your profile.

The key tenets of the elevator pitch are going to help you build a better introduction, whether you're delivering it in person, over video or in written format.

UPDATE THE CAREER PLANNING TOOL

Now that you are familiar with building your brand, it might be a good idea to go back and update your Career Planning Tool.

There are so many more opportunities for you to tell your story. But make sure you document your personal brand, identify the consistent components of your brand (key phrases for example), and the opportunities you want to use to broadcast your brand as part of your career plan.

KEY TAKEAWAYS

- Creating and maintaining your online brand is crucial since it will help you tell the right story when people look for you online.
- You should create a body of work to leverage all the online properties at your disposal and make sure you are telling a coherent and consistent story.
- Your elevator pitch is a great tool to help you differentiate yourself from others and set yourself up for more engagement.

PART E

EXECUTION

"The immature think that knowledge and action are different, but the wise see them as the same."

—*The Bhagavad Gita*

"In theory, there is no difference between practice and theory. In practice, there is."

—Yogi Berra

You have strategized. You have created an amazing career plan. You now have a blueprint for your future. You have made a decision and you are committed to it. You have defined a great personal brand that reflects your brand of leadership.

Now, the next step is to put the plan in motion and bring the strategy to life.

In this section which breaks down the **Elevate Step**, we will go over Elevate Leadership Flywheel which includes techniques to take your job performance to the next level and emerge as a successful leader. The objective is to start turning the flywheel, and as you make progress, you gain momentum with subsequent steps by telling your story effectively, building a great network, achieving new career opportunities, and learning new skills. Each step in the Elevate Leadership Flywheel automagically leads to the next and you build momentum toward a successful leadership career.

Unlike previous sections, all chapters in this section cover the activities of the **Elevate Step**. Let's learn more about the Elevate Leadership Flywheel first.

SOURCE: WWW.NAPKINSIGHTS.COM/NAPKIN/865/

CHAPTER 18

ELEVATE LEADERSHIP FLYWHEEL

"What we fear doing most is usually what we most need to do."

—Timothy Ferriss, *The 4 Hour Workweek*

That beautiful potted plant in your living room is growing every day because you have been taking care of it and watering it regularly. Eventually the plant gets to a size which is larger than the pot it's in. At that point, you realize that you need to put the plant in a larger pot because it has outgrown its current one.

As you take action and demonstrate leadership, you will outgrow your role. You will find yourself moving to bigger roles. All you did to make that happen was put the Elevate Leadership Flywheel in action, creating compounded growth for yourself.

The Elevate Leadership Flywheel creates compound results. Over a period of time, these results are massive. They create leadership opportunities for you. However, it is extremely important to have the right mindset for this journey.

The **Elevate Step** is the **most important** aspect of the 7 Steps Process, and you will need to invest maximum effort. The great work you do in your career sets the flywheel in motion and, like a chain reaction, everything else falls into place.

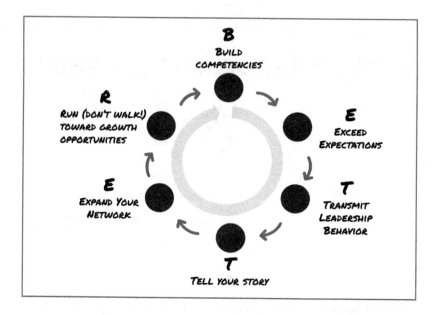

Each activity leads to the next and that's how you put the flywheel in motion to accelerate your career.

The Execution Section will demonstrate how you can do this great work and do justice to your skills and competencies. In short, how you can become a BETTER leader:

- Build competencies: develop career leadership skills
- Exceed expectations: create value and take your performance to the next level
- Transmit leadership behavior: demonstrate leadership
- Tell your story: help your personal brand shine
- Expand your network: develop connections
- Run (don't walk!) toward growth opportunities: identify new roles and capture opportunities

CHAPTER 19

BUILD COMPETENCIES

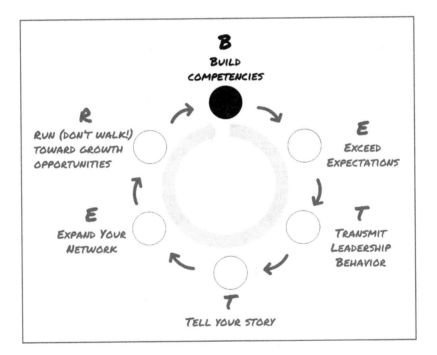

The Build Competencies Activity within the Elevate Leadership Flywheel is where you will become familiar with developing foundational career leadership skills.

The activity includes a curated collection of topics that are designed to help you succeed in the modern workplace right from day one:

- All aboard! First ninety days of your new role
- The number one skill to master
- Deliver great presentations
- Run meetings like a pro!
- Find those (elusive!) mentors
- Deal with negative feedback

ALL ABOARD! FIRST NINETY DAYS OF A NEW ROLE

The first ninety days of a new job or a new role hold great importance in your career. You have likely been through a tough interview process to successfully land a new job or a new role.

Your actions and interactions in these first ninety days will establish your leadership credibility and lay the foundation for your long-term working relationships.

As you work through your first ninety days, create and connect with the people with whom you are going to work. Your new colleagues have no idea who you are or what you've done before. This is an excellent opportunity for you to reestablish your personal brand in your new organization.

Make sure to enter those first ninety days with a game plan.

The ninety-day plan in your new job or new role follows the ILPA Framework, which has four components, **introduction, learn, plan, and act**. After introduction, the next three components – learn, plan, act – follow a logical order. Once your introduction is over, you should allocate roughly about thirty days for each of the remaining three stages. Ideally, these parts will take up the first ninety days of your new job.

Pro tip: In some cases, you might get into roles which require you to hit the ground running pretty much immediately. No need to panic, you can still deploy this framework, however, the learn, act, and plan steps will overlap quite a bit.

I STANDS FOR INTRODUCTION

Your introduction is your narrative and it's similar to the elevator pitch you've already crafted. What is the story you want to tell others at this new job? What you say should resonate with the values espoused by the company and more importantly, it should align with your values.

L STANDS FOR LEARN

First, learn about your role and your organization. You have to understand what role you've been hired to fill. During the interview, you would've been briefed about the responsibilities your new job entails. Do not shy away from asking for more details. Now that you are in the role, it is your prerogative to dig deep, and understand the expectations that come with the role. Only then can you exceed your employer's expectations.

In some cases, you might also have to reset your manager's expectations. The learning component of ILPA also includes understanding the purpose of your organization. What business are they involved in? What is the organization's strategy? How do they approach their business? Your job in this first phase is to listen intently.

Once you're done with your intro, listen and absorb as much information as you can about everything that's happening within the company.

Most importantly, learn more about the people working there. You need to determine the influencers and the stakeholders. Knowing the right people will help you when the time is right.

P STANDS FOR PLAN

The next component of the ninety-day plan is to ... well ... plan. Now that you've learned everything there is to know about your organization and imbibed the culture, you need to start to create your own plan. What are the things that you are going to do in the near future in your job? Plan out your strategy and goals for the next six, twelve, or even eighteen months in advance. When you reach those milestones, you can look back and evaluate yourself.

A STANDS FOR ACT

Act is all about execution. You've created a plan, and now it's time to execute it.

You cannot execute your plan without some level of cooperation from your colleagues.

And you cannot do this without understanding how your colleagues or manager work.

Start socializing with your stakeholders and figure out how it's best to work with them. What is their working style? What are some of their personal likes and dislikes? If there are limited opportunities for you to observe and understand your colleagues, get some help. Ask a trusted peer. In my experience, I've found executive assistants (EAs) to be a wealth of information in this space. Just a thirty-minute coffee meeting with an EA will provide you more than enough information in this area.

People who come into a new job or a new role usually do so with a fresh pair of eyes due to outside experience. When you come in with that outside-in view, you are in a better position to make calls on how projects run in your new company. Make sure you take note of all your observations. It could be things like "the sales process seems to have too many unnecessary steps; this is an area of improvement in the future."

As you make these notes, make sure to document them using OneNote or Evernote as you might need to reference these. Your fresh insights have the power to breathe new life into a broken process or a stagnant project.

At the end of the ninety days, you should be able to do a couple of things successfully:

- Introduce yourself and articulate your organizational purpose and strategy.
- Share a work plan that will help execute your organization's strategy.

The "learn, plan, act" portion of a ninety-day plan may be reduced to a thirty-day plan for organizations that move really quickly. For others, it might take even longer to formulate the ILPA Framework. It depends on your organization's pace and culture.

KEY TAKEAWAYS

- The first ninety days at any new job or a new role are crucial to how you're perceived as an employee.
- Do not enter the ninety days without a plan of action. Use the ILPA Framework to navigate through those first three months.

THE NUMBER ONE SKILL TO MASTER

In general, all of us have four career phases – new college grad, early in your career, mid-career, and late career. As you go through these different stages, there is a specific skill that will not only help you get ahead in your career, but also uplevel your compensation and raise it to a point you'd never imagined it would go.

This number one skill is a combination of **communication and informal public speaking.**

Most executives around you – VPs, SVPs, and CEOs – have amazing communication and public speaking skills. They have their own style of communication and are highly successful in taking their ideas to their stakeholders and audience effectively. You may have the best ideas, the best design, or the best concepts in the world, but if they are not articulated and presented well, then they are of less use. So, if you want to take your thoughts, ideas, and your career to the next level, communication and public speaking are primary skills to possess.

Public speaking is the art of influence. In many companies, there is a complex organizational structure, and the art of influence will help you take your agenda forward.

So, how do you develop this skill? How do you learn to be a better communicator and a better public speaker?

A simple formula called LIP is the answer.

LIP has three steps – listen, improve/improvise, and practice.

LISTEN

There is a reason why the first step is to listen. To be an effective communicator and public speaker, you have to listen.

You need to go beyond just hearing others and listen intently. What are they saying? Where are they coming from? What prompts them to say what they say? If you listen intently and understand their perspective, you can be a better speaker.

IMPROVE/IMPROVISE

Be engaged in the conversation and ask relevant and intelligent questions. Remember, asking questions is also a form of communication. It often happens in a conversation that you may paraphrase others to clarify what you've heard. When you paraphrase, you can make sure that you've understood correctly what the other person or your audience is saying. You also connect with your audience effectively and get on the same wavelength so you can proceed to the next step in communication.

Here are a few tips on how to enhance your everyday workplace communication.

- **Figure out the audience and the context.** Understanding your audience is fundamental to communication. Who is in the audience? What do they care about? What is the context for this conversation?

- **Couch controversial topics.** Often, talking publicly, or giving presentations on controversial topics leads to tense situations. This is where you need to tread cautiously. The best way to approach these topics is to couch them. Couching is a form of communication in which you use words related to a suggestion, like "probably" or "possibly." Sometimes you have to use these soft words to bring up a new idea or a controversial topic.

- **Make it memorable.** Six months from now, your audience is not going to remember the specific details of the conversation you had with them. But what they will remember for sure is how you made them feel. Did you make your audience feel inclusive? Did you share a personal story? Did you create a connection?

PRACTICE

Sharing our thoughts, our perspectives, our concepts, and designs with different teams is work life du jour. Practicing on a continuous basis is how to get better at it.

You can practice in front of your team or a colleague and request live feedback.

Another way to practice is to do some recording. All of us have this wonderful device called the smartphone. Video record yourself and then analyze yourself speaking.

The answers to these questions will help you create the best impression in the audience's mind.

- What does your body language say?
- Are the words you're using effective?
- Are you making eye contact?
- Are you emphasizing the right words in your presentation or your speech?

KEY TAKEAWAYS

- Practice your everyday communication skills to better connect with your peers and superiors.
- Follow the LIP formula to become a great communicator.

Once you're onboarded and well on your way into your new job, it's important not to get too settled in it that you stagnate. Continuous evolution is as essential to exceeding expectations. More often than not, the power to make that happen is with you, rather than your manager.

HOW TO FIND THOSE (ELUSIVE) MENTORS

Mentors are extremely important for your career, and the value they bring to you cannot be stressed enough. Mentors help your career by providing advice, opening doors, and providing otherwise unattainable resources.

There are mentors you meet once or twice in your entire life, and then there are mentors with whom you have an ongoing relationship. Either way, think of them as counselors who are going to provide advice to you.

Mentors don't necessarily need to be executives or leaders. A mentor could be anybody who is smarter than you.

Mentors can be of two types: virtual and real.

Virtual mentors are people who are content producers like authors, bloggers, podcasters, and the like. They produce mass media and provide advice to people in general. Tim Ferriss is my prime example of a virtual mentor. He runs a great podcast on productivity and business called "The Tim Ferriss Show." Virtual mentors may or may not know you individually, but by consuming their media, you begin to see them as mentors who speak to you on a personal level. By downloading the knowledge that they provide, you are elevating your life across domains. Your ability to have virtual mentors is limitless.

On the other hand, real mentors are those in your close network who are willing to help and teach you.

Here are some things to keep in mind when looking for a real mentor:

1. Make sure they are in your network. Approaching complete strangers for guidance is a bit difficult. You should know your potential mentor on a first-name basis.

2. Mentors are generally people who like to help. So, you don't need to formally ask them to mentor you. It's implied.

3. When you're approaching mentors, figure out how you can return their investment of time and energy. If there is anything you can help a mentor with, you should do that. Once you help a mentor, you can request their help. The best way to approach mentors is to give them something, and then figure out the most diplomatic way to put your questions to them.
   Be clear about your request. Be clear about what you need. Is it a question about a resource? Is it a contact? Is there someone in their network to whom you need an introduction? You should be clear in your mind about what you're going to ask them, and it has to be actionable. Then you leave it to the mentor as to how they can help you.

4. Do not insist on an in-person meeting. Mentors are busy people, and they may not be able to make time in person, but they may do a quick phone call or video call with you, and that's still as good.

> Mentors don't necessarily need to be executives or leaders. A mentor could be anybody who is smarter than you in a particular area or on a particular topic.

MENTORING AND COACHING ARE DISTANT COUSINS

A coach is someone who helps you with tools and resources on an ongoing basis. On the other hand, a mentor is someone to whom you reach out for specific advice or expertise. A coach is someone who makes things explicit to you. Mentoring or mentorship is sometimes done by observation. A mentor could even be your own manager or people within your network with whom you're currently working. They may not know that they are a mentor to you, but you know that they are. Mentoring is observational a lot of times, whereas coaching is done one-on-one.

THANK THEM FOR THEIR HELP

Always let your mentor know your gratitude. Thank them for their advice and maintain contact with them as much as possible. The more you do that, the more engagement and relationship you're going to drive. Having a mentor who cares about your career success is a blessing. They are rare, but you can seek them out and get help from them, while contributing something in return.

KEY TAKEAWAYS

- Never underestimate the value of mentors in your career.
- Virtual mentors advise people in general through blogs, books, and podcasts.
- Real mentors are people in your network whom you can ask for help.
- Be clear in your request when you reach out to your mentors.
- Always thank your mentors for their help.

DEAL WITH NEGATIVE FEEDBACK

Often our reaction to negative feedback is to get defensive and deflect the blame away from us.

When we receive negative feedback, we might come up with excuses like, "I didn't do it," "It was not my fault," or we just blame it on "the system."

Rather than taking the blame on ourselves and taking responsibility for something that went wrong, we try to sidestep it.

But here's what you need to realize; negative feedback is a gift. When you get negative feedback, be thankful.

The person who's giving you the negative feedback could be your manager, a peer, or a colleague; it doesn't matter. Your reaction to it should be, "Tell me more."

You deal with negative feedback by *owning it*. You ask the other person, "How do you think I could have avoided that problem?" or "How do you think I could have addressed that situation in a better way?"

As you have that hard conversation about negative feedback, it opens up the problem, and then you understand the issue a little bit better. This is a much more valuable conversation to have rather than avoiding taking responsibility or deflecting blame.

Listen to the feedback, own it, take notes, and double down on the solution. After some time, go back to the person who gave you that feedback and show them how you've made progress on that particular issue.

> Negative feedback is an opportunity to learn something new about yourself and your role.

This is the fastest way to get into their good books after receiving negative feedback. They recognize you as a person who is not only listening, but also acting on that feedback. That is real learning. This also shows that you are a genuine person eager to make inroads into your career. People become very appreciative when you receive their feedback and respond to it constructively.

When you get back to people in this way, they tend to appreciate the effort you put into your work. It is a great way to build your professional network. This is how you turn negative feedback into a gift for yourself.

KEY TAKEAWAYS

- Be positive when faced with criticism. Show eagerness to correct your mistake and learn from the experience.
- Demonstrate your willingness to work on the feedback and come up with a solution.
- Earn appreciation through the effort you put in and build your professional network.

CHAPTER 20

EXCEED EXPECTATIONS

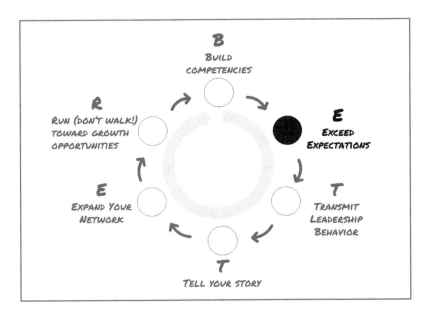

W hat is the fundamental challenge with job performance? Many people don't understand what is expected of them in their job. Many people who are in their jobs don't know what their manager or their organization is expecting from them. If you don't understand the expectation, you can't perform accordingly. If you're not performing to that unknown expectation, you are performing below par.

Exceeding the agreed-upon expectations is how you go from a mediocre performer in the company to an outstanding performer.

It's important to understand the specific expectations for your job and your role, and to exceed those expectations.

> Exceeding the agreed-upon expectations is how you go from a mediocre performer in the company to an outstanding performer.

FOUR ACTIONS TO THE NEXT LEVEL

There are four actions to take your job performance to the next level. There is a bonus action as well, so you get a prize! ☺

UNDERSTAND YOUR ROLE

The first step is to write down on a piece of paper what you believe your organization expects of you in your role: what your responsibilities are and how you will be measured in this job.

Identify your metrics and how you are going to be measured against others in the organization.

Having that information on a single sheet is probably the most important thing you can do. That's the first action that you have to take.

RESET EXPECTATIONS

The next one is slightly difficult, but very much doable. Once you understand the expectations of your role, the next step is for you to approach your manager and say, "I've been in this role for some time. I would like to make sure I understand your expectations really clearly." Sit down with your manager and go through your understanding of the role. You might be surprised to find that there are differences between what you think your role is and what your manager thinks your role is. So, it's important to get an understanding of the manager's and company's expectations of your role.

Here's the interesting part. You reset some of their expectations, so they are in alignment with your vision of your role. This puts you in a much better position to understand expectations, meet expectations, and also exceed expectations.

PERFORM

The third step is quite simple: perform. Once you know the expectations of your role, you've reset those expectations, and are on the same page with your manager, you have to perform in your role. *There is no shortcut to hard work.* You simply must perform. But here's the deal. As you perform, you will do much better now than prior years because you clearly understand what's expected of you.

EXCEED EXPECTATIONS

You know what's expected. Exceeding the agreed-upon expectations is how you go from a mediocre performer in the company to an outstanding performer. You perform and you exceed.

Let's take one of my clients, Joel, a salesperson, as an example. The best salespeople in business always exceed their sales goal, and Joel is no different. He negotiates the sales number he is expected to meet, making sure it's an achievable target. Then he exceeds that number. Every. Single. Time.

To others, Joel is a hero. A sales rockstar. I think he's more than that, he is the master of managing expectations. I can bet my top dollar that just this skill will enable him to take on more leadership roles in the near future.

Once you know what's expected, perform consistently to exceed those expectations.

AND NOW THE BONUS ACTION

As you outperform in your current role, show that you are performing at the next level as well. Demonstrate it with your body language and your expression. Sit up straight, pay attention, and be present in your interactions with your peers, your team, and your upper management.

You can also choose to change your wardrobe so that you are making an impression and creating a presence for yourself. But remember, having that presence without having performance is fluff. So be careful as you go down this path. The bonus action for you is to show outwardly how you're performing through your body language and through your presence.

Following these actions will help you develop a much better job performance and exceed the expectations your organization and your manager have of you.

KEY TAKEAWAYS

- Ask questions to exceed expectations
  Write down on a piece of paper what your responsibilities are. If there is any ambiguity, be sure to ask questions and then ask more questions until you're clear about them.
- Clear any confusion
  Once you know what is expected from you, sit down with your manager and make sure you're both on the same page. Any mismatch will cause many headaches farther down the line. You don't want to spend time on a time-consuming task only to be told by your manager that it wasn't your responsibility to begin with.
- Perform, perform, and perform
  There really is no shortcut here. You must simply perform well. Since you know and understand your role well, you can't blame anybody else for your lack of performance. Know what you're expected to do, and then exceed it.
- Show your passion
  Your passion for your job must be reflected in your personality as well. This is key. Most people simply perform and assume they'll get noticed. To truly exceed expectations, your body language must match your work ethic.

HOW TO MANAGE YOUR MANAGER AND MANAGING UPWARDS

One of the most critical relationships in a job is your relationship with your manager. Often, a bad relationship with a manager is the primary reason someone quits their job. So, managing your manager is a high-stakes game in your career.

But what is meant by managing your manager? And how do you do that?

If you're a manager, you manage downward. If you're leading people who are at a peer level to you, you're managing sideways. Managing your manager and your manager's manager is called managing upward.

Managing your manager is an essential part of anybody's job. More often than not, careers are made by employees learning to manage their managers better.

"My manager manages me. Do I get to manage my manager?" If this is your current thought, then let me just make something clear – you both manage each other. For this reason, it is super crucial for you to manage your team and your manager.

Let's look at how exactly you go about doing this essential relationship management.

UNDERSTAND EXPECTATIONS

Understanding what your manager expects from you is extremely important because he/she always measures and analyzes you against the expectations they have for you whenever you're having an interaction with them. So, make sure you understand your manager's expectations about your work, performance, and roles as clearly as you can.

UNDERSTAND YOUR MANAGER'S WORK STYLE

Does your manager like a lot of details or do they not? Do they prefer verbal communication to written communication? It is critical to understand the work style of your manager really well so that you can work better with them. It makes communication easier and improves work compatibility and thought partnership. It will also help you build credibility and trust with your manager.

ESTABLISH A TRUST-BASED RELATIONSHIP

One of the most essential things for managers is to have a trusted relationship with their employees. You can build trust with your manager by consistently delivering tasks on or before deadline. You must exceed quality and even expectations that your manager sets, which will establish credibility and trust with them.

MAKE SURE THERE ARE NO SURPRISES

One of the most significant practices smart people use to keep a manager's trust is to make sure there are no surprises. Most managers have this unwritten rule with their team, which is, "No surprises, please!" So, if you come up with unexpected situations, make sure you provide them with a heads-up so that there are no surprises.

If you, unfortunately, create a surprise for your manager, it might lead to credibility issues, lack of trust and loss in your manager's confidence in you. One way to avoid surprises is to have a 360-degree view for your work to identify potential challenges and blind spots.

Another way is to share the risks and potential challenges with the manager upfront. Once you have brought it to their attention, it can longer be a surprise.

ASK CLARIFYING QUESTIONS: THEY MIGHT EVEN HELP YOUR MANAGER

Ask questions. It always helps to ask questions to clarify things and get adequate information about your projects. Sometimes these questions even help your manager because they might develop a clearer perception of the job in hand that will allow both of you to be sure there are no assumptions.

HELP YOUR MANAGER SEE OVER THE HORIZON

One of the critical things in managing and working with your manager is to help them see over the horizon. Give your manager a 360-degree view based on what you see. Your manager needs to understand your tasks in hand. Sharing a view of your work and projects with your manager plays a vital role in delivering a successful outcome.

LOOK OUT FOR YOUR MANAGER

Make it clear that you are there to make them even more successful. Even though your manager has gotten to where they are because they've been successful, your job is to make them even more so. It's a two-way street. Look out for them, and your manager will look out for you.

ASK YOUR MANAGER FOR HELP

There is no shame in asking for help from your manager. Asking for help enables you to establish a great working relationship with your manager. Asking for help is a sign of strength. It indicates that you feel comfortable in that trust-based relationship with your manager.

KEY TAKEAWAYS

- Make sure you understand your manager's expectations.
- Understand the work style of the manager.
- Make sure there are no surprises.
- Deliver great work.
- Look out for your manager and make your manager even more successful.

CHAPTER 21

TRANSMIT LEADERSHIP BEHAVIOR

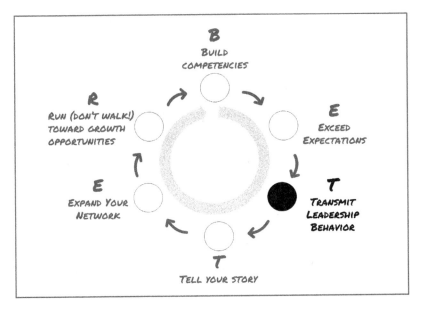

Work is hectic. Work is charged. Work rarely gives you the luxury to invest time in introspection. Yet, one of the most essential topics for introspection in your career is status quo versus change. Sometimes, you have to stop in your tracks for a moment and think about the positive changes you're driving in your space.

SEVEN SUPERPOWERS TO DEMONSTRATE LEADERSHIP

There are seven career superpowers that help you challenge the status quo in your work environment and become a change agent. It is likely that you already have these superpowers. It might be just a matter of honing these skills.

Often, even the best of us fail to identify our skills and experience.

In other words, you may not realize that you have these superpowers within you. It is always good to take a step back, and understand:

- What are your superpowers?
- How can you amplify your skills to create more value not only for your career, but also for your organization?

All of these superpowers are important, some more than others. Let's go through this list where it leads up to the most important superpower.

SUPERPOWER #7: FOCUS

Superpower number seven is about focus. The world has gone digital, creating a constant "noise" around you: social media, emails, text messages, constant meetings, and conversations.

Your superpower in this space is how you separate from the noise and identify a clear signal. Focusing in a constantly distracted world is a superpower.

Separate out all the noise around you and focus on your objective. For example, it could be as simple as turning on the airplane mode on your phone to stop any notifications during important times of the day. Or it could be blocking your calendar for deep, focused work with your team or by yourself.

Creating focus and clarity for yourself and your team becomes a superpower. Exercise this superpower to work on the objectives you've laid down for yourself and your team.

SUPERPOWER #6: COMMUNICATION

Yes, this is a clichéd topic. Without question, everyone needs to have great communication skills. However, communication is not just about speaking well, it's also about listening well.

We have two ears and one mouth for good reason! We are expected to listen well, think deeply about what was said, and then speak in a way that engages others. This is how great communication skills become your superpower.

Having open and clear communication with those around you will help achieve better results for your team. Especially when working in a team environment, it helps to listen intently and be transparent in our communication with each member of the team.

SUPERPOWER #5: DECISION-MAKING

Yes, decision-making is a superpower, and perhaps one of the most essential.

Good decision-making skills are important tools in your toolbox as a professional. As a stepping stone, you can build mental models to guide you through tough decisions.

Think of mental models as frameworks that will help you make a higher quality decision at work. The interesting part is, as you grow in your career and gain more experience, you learn more mental models. You start identifying patterns that match mental models, gradually elevating yourself to a situation where you make tough decisions using a specific mental model or a combination of models.

A lot of times, when it comes to mental models, it's about pattern recognition. Can you recognize certain patterns and then start applying mental models toward those patterns?

The first example of a mental model is the Pareto Principle. The Pareto Principle says not everything in life is evenly distributed and that roughly 80 percent of the effects come from 20 percent of the causes aka the 80-20 rule.

Some would even say that it means that life is not fair.

20 percent of the input creates 80 percent of the results. Or in your company, it's possible that 20 percent of the professionals are actually creating 80 percent of the results. Or 20 percent of your customers are bringing in 80 percent of the revenue. Again, this is not an exact answer, but what it gives you is a sense of the input that creates maximum output. If you apply that to your career, you can think about it as 20 percent of my skills create 80 percent of the results.

This means if you can find out what those 20 percent things are, you should spend your energy on doubling down or even tripling down on them.

The second example of a mental model is the 10/10/10 rule.

We often find ourselves faced with a massive decision in our lives. Should I take that job? Should I relocate to another part of the country for better opportunities? Should I marry that person or should I take up this particular career?

This is where the 10/10/10 rule really helps.

There are three bullet points that you have to consider for 10/10/10 decision-making.

- If I take this decision, what will be the consequences of this in about 10 minutes?
- If I take this decision, what would be the consequences of this decision in 10 months?
- If I take this decision, what would be the consequences of this decision in 10 years?

By applying this tool, you're really thinking through not just the short-term or medium-term consequences but the long-term consequences as well.

For example, here's how you use this tool if you're on the verge of taking up a new job:

- In the next 10 minutes, you will be signing the appointment letter and it's going to feel good because it's a new beginning and new opportunities.
- In the next 10 months, you'll reach a certain level of compensation that you're comfortable with. You'll be settled in and life will be good.

But 10 years from now, will this new job really accelerate your career or will it make it stagnant? Will it help you learn new things, continuously upskill and boost your career trajectory?

If yes, then you should take that job. If not, then you should keep looking.

That job may look tempting and it may look like the shiny new thing that you want to be a part of, but it may not be the right thing for you in the long-term.

So a model like the 10/10/10 rule allows you to make decisions – short, medium and long term – that really takes the emotion out of the decision and helps you make really good objective decisions in your life and in your career.

Let me give you two additional resources for decision-making.

One is a book by Ray Dalio titled *Principles*. Ray Dalio is one of the world's richest people, and he runs the world's largest hedge fund. He turned his mistakes and learnings into a set of principles that we can apply to our work lives. The second resource is *When*, a book by Dan Pink, in which he talks about the best time for making a decision. Timing is a crucial variable in decision-making. Dan uses data to recommend the best timing of different types of decisions.

SUPERPOWER #4: INFLUENCING

Influencing is different from communication. Influencing is different from engagement.

Doing the right thing is always the right thing. Influencing is how you can move other people toward a point of view that you know is right.

Influencing could involve many different things or persuade people to embrace your perspective. It's a combination of having the right narrative, the right visuals, and the right data, and packaging them into a single message for your stakeholders, your team, and your customers. The objective is to nudge them to do a few things:

1. Understand your point of view
2. Acknowledge that they have understood your point of view ☺
3. Be open to considering moving to your point of view

The last point is very important. One example of nudging them toward your point of view could be asking a question like "What will make you consider this?" or "If we were to move forward with this, will you consider working with me / us on it?"

Your influencing superpower helps you communicate your ideas more effectively and drive a better outcome. The power of influence is significant in today's corporate environment, especially if you're in dotted line relationships, where influencing others when you don't have authority becomes more relevant.

Your ability to influence also helps you create your own personal brand because the person who can convey his/her ideas the best way wins. This is an economy of ideas, so take your influencing superpower to the next level to push your ideas farther, make real change, and create more value for your team.

SUPERPOWER #3: ADAPTABILITY

Adaptability means we are pliant enough to adapt as needed to the continuous changing conditions of our current lives.

Things are changing so dynamically in the business and technological worlds it is almost unbelievable. The pace is only going to increase. You have to equip yourself to adapt to these fluctuating business dynamics and technology advances.

Here are some steps that might help you with work adaptability:

1. **Understand the change to anticipate it**: Using market exercises in the Preparation Part and the 3 Horizons Tool, you can develop awareness of market trends before these trends occur in your immediate environment.

2. **Account for change and learning**: Since change is the only constant in our work lives, allocate some time and money to learn new skills and gain new experience. These new skills will make your adaptation much easier and sustainable.

You need to adapt to accommodate dynamic trends and lead the change rather than be impacted by it. You have the power to take advantage of trends by turning those trends into tailwinds for you that propel your career forward, rather than making them headwinds for your career.

SUPERPOWER #2: EMPATHY

Empathy means you are capable of understanding what another person is experiencing or feeling; you can walk a mile in their shoes. That someone else could be your customer, a team member, or a subordinate. It could even be your life partner. Empathy helps you understand where they're coming from, and their pains and constraints. Understanding the pain of your stakeholders, your customers, and your employees gives you the opportunity to grasp the problem better and more meaningfully. This understanding leads to a better solution. Empathy is a massive superpower because you can understand what is driving the other person or the team.

SUPERPOWER #1: LEARNING

The number one superpower that will transform you into an agent of change is lifelong learning, and it is a superpower for a good reason. By continuously learning, we can build an unbeatable career stack. As we discussed, today's market is changing so fast that you need to constantly adapt. You have to constantly learn, too. Education happens in multiple ways. In general, there are three different ways to learn.

- **Audio**: we learn by listening to others
- **Visual**: we learn by seeing or observing
- **Kinesthetics**: we learn by doing

As we gain more experience, learning by doing becomes more important. We can build our career stack not only by listening and observing, but also by doing. Build a learning muscle for continuous education to enrich your talent stack. You will not only have a successful career, but you'll also have so many options in your career that you will have a hard time figuring out which opportunity to pursue.

> **KEY TAKEAWAYS**
> - Challenge the status quo by being an agent of change and driving in positive changes in your organization.
> - These seven superpowers to charge your career are already within you intrinsically, but you may not have realized it.
> - Identify these superpowers within you, amplify them, and use them regularly to develop your leadership skills.

HOW TO DEVELOP (AND KEEP) EXECUTIVE RELATIONSHIPS

Building a great working relationship with executives can help your career in many ways. It boosts your professional health and career longevity. Executives can influence the results of your project or your work.

Executives are excellent network enhancers. The more executives you have in your professional network, the better off you are. They can open up new career opportunities for you, because they are probably aware of industry trends, company news, and other key pieces of information such as unique hiring needs in their organizations which you may privy to. They do hold the keys to a lot of professional opportunities.

Executives play a crucial role in your next job search. If you're looking for your next opportunity, whether within your company or outside, these relationships will provide a good reference for your next position.

WHO ARE THESE EXECUTIVES?

Usually, executives hold positions of director and above, but are most likely vice presidents and above. They share certain characteristics:

- They're generally quite smart!
- They're great communicators.
- They're wonderful team builders and amazing leaders who inspire others to do better.
- They like to act, and they make quick and effective decisions.
- They're great with numbers and are capable of both quantitative and qualitative discussions about their business.
- Most importantly, they do not have much time on their hands. Their calendars are perpetually full.

HOW DO YOU BUILD GREAT RELATIONSHIPS WITH EXECUTIVES?

Here are some points to consider before attempting to build a strong network with them.

Connect with them as a human being. Building relationships with executives as human beings is essential. Stronger executive relationships help you become comfortable working with them and makes them more comfortable working with you.

If you have a meeting with an executive, **always arrive ahead of time.** Not only does this show good leadership, but it also demonstrates you're ready for the meeting and you value their time. It also allows some time for small talk, which is an essential aspect of networking.

Have a valuable conversation with executives. Most executives are busy and usually value only a productive interaction. If you have something you can share that they might not know about the business, that is something of value. Executives focus on measurements such as market share and customer opinion, as well as the health of the organization. What new perspective can you bring to those aspects of their business?

You should **always be able to answer the question, "So what?"** So, what if there's an issue? So, what if there's an opportunity? You should be able to synthesize the topic and answer the question.

Running a business is a numbers game. **Numbers and metrics are super important to executives.** The information you are sharing or presenting should include numbers which will make your topic much more valuable to an executive because numbers and metrics are quantifiable and understandable. Commentary about a business that comes along with numbers makes the information much more powerful.

When an executive reaches out to you over email or message, **your level of responsiveness must be much higher than usual.** It's not recommended to keep an email from an executive unread in your inbox for over forty-eight hours. If you don't have the information they're seeking at hand, make sure you at least respond with, "Thanks for the email, I'm going to look into this. I'll get back to you by X date." This way, they'll know you're aware of their query, and you're working on it. If you leave them hanging for too long, they'll go to someone else for help, and you'll have lost a potential opportunity to build your network.

Executives find problems challenging and often like to analyze them. **Think about how you can present problems as**

opportunities to improve. In other words, executives prefer opportunities over problems. Don't just tell them what the problems are. Always give them possible solutions and outcomes. Try to answer questions like, "What's the opportunity to improve?" and "How can we do this better?" You may not have the specific answers but even having an approach to come up with the answer will help your personal brand with executives. They will see you as a leader and not just as someone who is going to "do the work."

Keep a twenty to thirty second summary of what you're doing in mind. If you meet an executive in the elevator and they ask you, "Hey, what are you up to?" and you're tongue-tied or not able to articulate your ideas, then you're losing out on a huge chance to network. Executives are often interested in what you're doing and to understand the value you're creating. They are invested in connecting the dots within the organization. Information on your project will help them connect the dots and apply that intelligence to another part of the organization. They may even be able to connect you with people in the organization whose project visions align with yours. Just like that, you've strengthened your network.

KEY TAKEAWAYS

- Connect with executives with valuable and solution-driven conversations.
- A good introduction will give you credibility and help you engage with executives more effectively.
- Provide as much valuable information about yourself as possible in a short and concise introduction.

MANAGE DOTTED LINE REPORTING RELATIONSHIPS

There is a common question in professional life which has perplexed the best of us. How do you manage a dotted line reporting structure? How do you go about handling these vague relationships and to leverage them to benefit your career?

Before we get into how to manage a dotted line reporting structure, let's understand a bit more about it.

A dotted line relationship is an informal reporting relationship that can have a short or long duration. In any organization, especially large ones, you have a direct chain of command, where you report to someone, and that person reports to someone else. In a direct chain of command, the rules of the road are clearly established. What does your role entail? What does your manager expect from you? You have a clear line of vision into the expectations of your job and how you need to work with your manager or anyone in the hierarchy above and below you.

However, in large companies, multiple functions and practice areas have to work with each other. You need to get the work done using different functions within the same company. Dotted line relationships are formed because all these teams have to work together in an ad hoc or new project structure. The relationships you develop outside your direct line of reporting become extremely important for the success of your project as well as for your career.

Three important activities help you manage a dotted line relationship:

1. Understand team roles.
2. Put currency in the bank.
3. Ask for help.

It's important for you to understand how to manage these relationships well because they are much different from a direct manager relationship.

1. UNDERSTAND TEAM ROLES

One of the concepts that you should master is how to quickly grasp the functions of other team members and their roles. These people may be peers, on a higher level, or subordinate to you. You need to understand your team members':

- Titles
- Roles
- Functions
- Driving factors
- How they are measured

Understanding these things will give you a clearer idea of how to engage with them.

2. PUT CURRENCY IN THE BANK

Another concept in managing dotted line relationships is currency. Relationship currency is quite simply helping others and getting help from others, a way to make sure you can get things done. You extend your influence in the company as you build your network and unlock future career opportunities by managing dotted line relationships.

"Putting currency in the bank" translates to engaging with those who are in dotted line relationships with you, those to whom you are informally reporting or someone who is informally reporting to you. You can develop relationships proactively by helping them with their projects or key areas of work and regularly sharing information with them. When you help them by leveraging your strengths, you bring value to them. When you bring value to others, you put currency in their bank for yourself during future work.

You can put currency in the bank in multiple ways: provide advice, assist them in their work based on your area of expertise, open up your network for them, etc. Anything you can do to help them puts that currency in the bank.

3. ASK FOR HELP FROM DOTTED LINE RELATIONSHIPS

This step is the most fun step! You can tap into the currency you put in others' banks by asking for help when you need it.

If you're stuck in a project, or need extra hands to get something done, you can reach out to dotted line relationships for help. Managing these relationships helps you not just in your current role, but it has an impact on your overall career. When you are ready to change jobs in the near future, you can tap into these dotted line relationships and build your network as you search for new opportunities. Effectively managing dotted line relationships helps you accelerate your career by unlocking new career opportunities because your dotted line colleagues will be happy to recommend you as they change jobs.

KEY TAKEAWAYS

- A dotted line reporting structure is informal with vaguely established rules.
- To manage a dotted line relationship, you need to understand team roles, create value for others in the relationship, and ask for help when needed.
- Managing dotted line relationships opens up new opportunities and accelerates your career growth.

HOW TO DEAL WITH OFFICE POLITICS AND EMERGE AS A TRUE LEADER

Office politics are everywhere regardless of the company size, the industry it is in, or where it is located. You can choose to participate in office politics, or you can choose to stay away from it. But you just can't ignore it. Because companies are made of human beings, and where there are human beings, there will always be politics.

Here is how you can deal with office politics, address them in a professional way, and emerge as a leader.

> Show leadership by keeping yourself above politics.

By staying above office politics, you can demonstrate that you are completely about leading rather than following. Demonstrate that you are an objective leader by turning a negative conversation in the opposite direction.

In spite of taking the high road, there will be thorny and controversial discussions. They can't be side-stepped. Here are some ways to bring objectivity and leadership to a conversation when you are dealing with political topics in the office.

APPROACH POLITICS THROUGH A CUSTOMER LENS

An approach you can use to help yourself and your team figure out the right thing to do is ask what a customer would think. "What is the customer perspective on this topic?" The customer is always right because they are the reason your company is in business.

Having a customer's perspective and getting an understanding of how this topic affects customers is a great way to get above office politics.

MAKE DATA YOUR FRIEND

A recommended approach to be objective and clear about a controversial topic is to make data and facts your friend. Whenever you're dealing with politics, whenever you're dealing with gossip, whenever you're dealing with posturing from other people, think about how you can make your communication clear and fact-based.

Always ask yourself, "What's the right thing to say given these data points and facts?"

Making data and facts a part of your DNA will help you get above office politics and put yourself above hearsay and gossip.

TAKE THE "WHOLE COMPANY" PERSPECTIVE

Just like you looked at politics from the customer perspective, consider a point from the perspective of the whole company to determine the right thing to do.

Leaders often optimize a decision to better suit a specific function within a company. This might come at the expense of another function, which destroys value across the company.

Here's what will happen as you move out of office politics and emerge as a fact-based, objective leader: you will create a great personal brand. The more you rely on data, the more you rely on facts, the more your personal brand will run on steroids.

You can position yourself for the next level by demonstrating you are neutral to office politics and that your true objective is oriented toward what's best for the company and its customers.

Doing this presents many advantages:

- By removing yourself from office politics, you don't get entangled in it.

- By aligning yourself to company objectives, you are helping the company's strategy and also helping customers.
- Being an objective neutral party helps to build your personal branding, which will help your trajectory.

KEY TAKEAWAYS

- You can't ignore office politics, but you can rise above it.
- By rising above office politics, you demonstrate you are an objective leader.
- Take the customer's perspective when dealing with office politics.
- Data and facts are your best friends in controversial situations.
- Always think about how a decision affects the whole company.

DELIVER GREAT PRESENTATIONS

Delivering presentations is a core skill for leaders. Delivering a speech is about presenting data points and arguments, but above all, it is about telling a story. People engage more effectively when they hear a story.

A great presentation consists of two equal parts – creation and delivery. If you're lacking in either, your presentation may not have the impact you'd like.

CREATE PRESENTATIONS THAT LEAVE A LASTING IMPACT

Most presentations have a firehose quality, with the audience sitting through hours of data presented in a lackluster format. We rarely remember what was shared, leaving the time we spent listening anything but productive. Your presentations must have the ability to captivate the audience as well as communicate something valuable to them effectively. It is not an unattainable task.

KNOW YOUR AUDIENCE

Presentations at meetings, at live events, or over video are set up with a topic and an audience in mind. Your job is to figure out who that audience is, what level of expertise they have, what they represent, and most importantly, what they care about.

If you know what they care about, then you will be aware of the biases they may have. This helps you weave the presentation in a manner that really draws your audience into the conversation and helps them make better decisions.

BUILD YOUR STORYLINE

Start your presentation with the answer. This is a slightly controversial idea. I've been through numerous presentations where the presenter gradually builds up the story for forty-five minutes and then gives the answer. A lot of us make this mistake. We've been trained to provide the answer at the end. Do not do this. The first thing your storyline should start with is the answer.

For example, you can start off your presentation by stating the problem and then saying, "We are proposing X, Y, and Z as the responses to this problem. Here's why." It will draw in your audience and get them invested in your idea.

This technique is best summarized by the acronym BLUF – Bottom Line Up Front.

This simply means that you provide the answer at the start of the presentation before providing supporting information.

An outstanding framework for structuring presentations is the Minto Pyramid Principle[15]. Barbara Minto's work is a great reference for anyone looking for a framework to present their ideas and take their presentations to the next level.

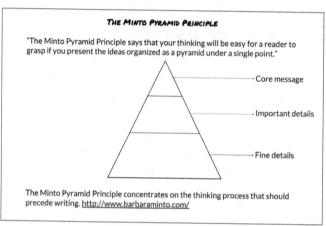

When you create a great business presentation, think about the Minto Pyramid. At the peak of the pyramid is the core message or the answer you want to share with your participants. The mid-section of the pyramid comprises the supporting data for your answer. At the bottom of the pyramid lie the details. As you craft a presentation, think about the pyramid – the actual core, which is the message that you want to deliver, followed by the supporting data, and then the finer details that you want to tell. Often, the details supporting your data can be moved to the appendix, but your stakeholders are here for the answer so give that to them first.

USE SYNTHESIS TO AVOID "DEATH BY POWERPOINT"

It's not uncommon for a presenter to keep showing slide after slide

---

15 Minto, Barbara, *The Minto Pyramid Principle: Logic in Writing and Thinking* (Minto International, Inc., 1987, ISBN: 978-0960191024)

without answering the question, "So what?" One way you can avoid this mistake is by using the power of synthesis. Synthesis means your slide, or your message should answer the question, "So what?"

For example, you can make the statement, "Smartphone usage across the world has gone up by 80 percent." This statement by itself does not mean much unless you give your audience the "So what?" of it. You should be able to tell them why that statement is important and why it's relevant to the meeting. The relevance of a conversation should be reflected in your content. In the smartphone usage example, the "So what?" could be "Billions of people now have access to powerful applications. This is an irreversible trend to provide technological access to people living in even the most remote areas and connecting them to mainstream markets." This synthesis or takeaway makes your point sharper and creates an impact for your presentation.

> When you're presenting your storyline, whether on a whiteboard or via slides, make sure there's a flow to the story.

REHEARSE

Rehearsal is extremely important when you're delivering a big presentation. Rehearse in your own office or at home in front of a mirror. Record yourself on camera to rehearse how you look and how you sound.

Your audience will judge you based on the tone of your voice and on how you present yourself. Use your smartphone to record your tone, correct your posture, and fine tune your delivery. This audiovisual component plays an important role along with the actual content and the data that you want to share.

Use power poses to get into top mental and physical state before an important presentation. Fifteen minutes before the presentation, find a private place and practice some power poses.

> Use power poses to get into top mental and physical shape before an important presentation.

In her book, *Presence*, Amy Cuddy explores the benefits of mimicking the body language of powerful people. She argues that power-posing can be more effective than traditional confidence-boosting exercises, like telling yourself how great you are.

She describes power poses as expansive and open. When you adopt one, you take up a lot of space and hold your arms and legs away from your body.

For example, in "The Wonder Woman" power pose, you stand with your feet apart, your hands on your hips, and your chin tilted upward.

Power posing in front of a mirror before a key presentation has been shown to create positive changes in emotional, cognitive, behavioral, and physiological responses while lowering cortisol levels in the blood[16]. This gives you the feeling of being more confident. It also

---

16 Amy Cuddy, Caroline A. Wilmuth, Andy J. Yap, Dana Carney, "Preparatory Power Posing Affects Nonverbal Presence and Job Interview Performance," Journal of Applied Psychology, February 2015, https://www.researchgate.net/publication/272097010_Preparatory_Power_Posing_Affects_Nonverbal_Presence_and_Job_Interview_Performance

allows you to get more air into your diaphragm and helps you deliver your talk in a very commanding tone.

MAKE THE AUDIENCE FEEL: GIVE A GIFT

A long time from now, your audience is likely not going to remember what you presented. But they will remember how you made them feel. Did you make them feel that you're leading them toward growth and progress? Did you make them feel that you're influencing them in the right direction? Or did you put your audience into a position where they're going to experience some fear or some confusion?

Think about what you want to make your audience feel. One technique to make your audience feel positive toward you and your idea is to determine the gift that you're giving them.

What gift do you have to offer your audience?

Are you giving them new insights? A new concept? Are you promising them new business?

Work your audience before and during the presentation. A few minutes before the presentation, go to the audience, engage with them, shake hands with them, and make sure they feel comfortable toward you and you are comfortable with them. During the presentation, go into the audience and call out individual people to get the conversation going.

Your audience always appreciates value. If you're not providing value, they will go back to their Facebook, Twitter, or whatever catches their fancy on their smartphones!

START STRONG, PROVIDE SOLID INFORMATION, AND FINISH STRONGER

Start your presentation by introducing the topic rather than introducing yourself.

For example, start with, "We all know we have a problem with our usage of mobile phone applications." The audience nods their heads in agreement. Now, you have a strong start with the core of the message, and you have managed to engage with the audience.

> We live in a world full of ideas and innovation. Unless you delight your audience with a captivating insight, don't expect them to buy in on your ideas. People who are more successful have an ability to influence others based on their ideas and their concepts.

As you go farther into your presentation, provide supporting data for your thesis and your answer. Be open to taking questions from the audience as well.

Do not schedule your Q&A at the end of your presentation. This is a very common mistake that people make. It can be depressing to hear "crickets chirping" when you finish your presentation and ask the audience, "Any questions?"

And yet, what do you do when there are no questions from the audience?

Have a backup question and present it as an interesting thought that you just had. For example, you go, "Okay. Seems like there are no questions for this presentation. But what do you think would happen if we implement this idea? Let me share a little bit more information on that with you."

Here, you've manufactured a question, planted a thought into their minds, and managed to drive more interaction.

But don't end just yet. Start off strong with the core message, then dive into the details with a bit of Q&A peppered in between, and you'll end even stronger.

The best example of this is Steve Jobs' keynote addresses. He always ended them with, "Oh, and one more thing[17]." What he said after that statement delighted the audience. In fact, the audience would start cheering in anticipation even before he could reveal what the "one thing" was. They had gotten so used to his strong finishes that they knew they wouldn't be disappointed.

End your presentation with one more thing, one more piece of data, one more idea, or one more concept that will leave your audience delighted. That's where you end the presentation – on delight.

---

17 Carmine Gallo, 'The Art of the Elevator Pitch,' Harvard Business Review, October 3, 2018, https://hbr.org/2018/10/the-art-of-the-elevator-pitch.

KEY TAKEAWAYS

- Always understand your audience before you create your presentation.
- Start your presentation with the answer. Make sure each slide answers the question, "So what?"
- Rehearse well before you deliver your presentation.
- Create a lasting impression in the minds of the audience.
- Keep BLUF in mind when creating presentations. Always give your audience the Bottom-Line Up Front (BLUF). Do not make them wait till the end of an hour-long meeting to give them the answer.
- Power posing is an amazing psychological hack you can use to boost your confidence before any presentation. Practicing this has been shown to lower cortisol levels in the blood.

RUN MEETINGS LIKE A PRO!

Meetings are a part of corporate life. You cannot run away from them. Running productive meetings so your audience benefits from it is an essential skill.

DO YOU REALLY NEED THAT MEETING?

But sometimes, meetings are huge time sinks.

As you prepare for the next meeting, think about its purpose. For example, the purpose could be to provide certain information, give a status update, make a decision, or even to have a negotiation. Since meetings have many different forms, it's important for you to understand a particular meeting's purpose. Once you have a clear idea of the reason for the meeting, it's time to ask the question, "Do I really need to have a meeting for this?"

> The best meeting is when a meeting does not happen.

Time is your most important non-renewable resource. If you can figure out alternative ways to provide the update or make the decision – maybe over email, instant messenger, or with a good old-fashioned phone call – and avoid having a meeting, that is the best meeting of all.

Considering the number of people in a typical meeting, their salaries, and other compensations, meetings could turn out to be expensive in the long run. Schedule a meeting, inviting solely the necessary people, only if you're sure it is vital to do so.

THE PRE-MEETING STRATEGY

How can you make the meeting better even before the meeting has started?

STATE THE OBJECTIVE ON THE AGENDA

Often, we become too focused on creating an agenda for the meeting. Agendas are important, no doubt. But defining a clear objective should take priority over any agenda.

An objective and agenda are two different things. The objective is the reason you are having a meeting, perhaps the result you hope to obtain, and the agenda is the way you're going to structure the meeting.

For example, an objective could be, "We are having a meeting to decide on X, Y, or Z."

There must be clarity on the meeting's purpose before you begin to build a structure for it. As a best practice, you can publish the objective and the agenda beforehand as part of your meeting invite. This gives people time to do research and be prepared to optimize the meeting time.

SEND OUT PRE-READING MATERIAL

In some companies like Amazon, the person who calls the meeting is required to publish a six-pager before the meeting is called. The six-pager provides the audience with information on the meeting before it happens. By doing this, everybody is aware of the context and the agenda for the meeting.

Any reading material that you want the participants to read prior to the meeting has to be delivered at least a couple of days before. By doing this, everybody is aware of the context and the agenda for the meeting.

KNOW YOUR PARTICIPANTS

Make a list of participants and think about how you are going to address them. What is their role in this meeting? If there are participants who have no role in the meeting, don't invite them.

How are they going to participate? Are they going to provide any crucial information? Are they going to consume information? Are they going to provide an opinion, perspective, or decision? Are they influencers or stakeholders? Know your participants' roles before sending them an invite.

ASSIGN A NOTE-TAKER

Note-taking during a meeting is an important element that many people neglect. Assign a note-taker before the meeting starts and let them know what their role entails.

IN-MEETING STRATEGY

If you called for a meeting, it's your job to provide context and background. People coming into a meeting usually have an idea of what to expect, but sometimes they might be busy or running late and they might miss the pre-meeting briefing. You can't really blame them. It happens to the best of us. In such instances, it is important to provide context and background as soon as you start your meeting. Remind the participants why they're there.

TAKE NOTES

Note-taking during a meeting is an important element that many people neglect. Taking notes, setting action items, and defining next steps are important parts of any meeting. If nobody has been designated to take notes, then that responsibility falls upon you. These notes are the main ingredient of a post-meeting strategy.

KEEP TRACK OF TIME

A very useful strategy that doesn't get used much in meetings is the use of a time cop. A time cop is a person who keeps the time and makes sure that the discussion moves forward. Time cops keep participants on task and engaged with the discussion.

AVOID MEETINGS BEING HIJACKED

No meetings are immune from being hijacked. Someone inevitably comes up with a topic that derails the entire discussion. The best way to avoid this is by creating a parking lot. Create a parking lot either on the whiteboard or in your notes, and politely let the participant know because their points aren't exactly relevant to the topic at hand, they have been moved to the parking lot. Topics in the parking lot are for the participants to resolve offline outside the meeting.

By creating a parking lot, you're creating space for other people to have the conversation after the meeting, and at the same time you get your meeting back on track.

DISBAND THE MEETING AT THE RIGHT TIME

If you had initially scheduled a one-hour meeting but find that you've taken care of the meeting objective within twenty minutes, let everybody go. Once you're done with the objective of the meeting, you don't need to use the entire hour.

The participants will appreciate you giving them time back on their calendars.

> Time is the most important non-renewable resource that you have at your disposal.

WHAT HAPPENS POST-MEETING?

Thank the attendees for their time and their participation.

But most importantly, send out the meeting notes, action items, and next steps within twenty-four hours of the end of the meeting while it's still fresh in people's minds. Drive engagement by asking the participants to point out if the meeting met its objective or if any topic wasn't discussed enough. Ask them if the notes you shared capture the most important ideas of the meeting.

When you make decisions in meetings, it's only a verbal commitment. But when you send out an email with notes, that notification is the real handshake. That is the contract. The notes provide you with the basis to claim, "Yes, this was agreed upon in the meeting, and this is our contract."

Notes provide a sense of closure for the meeting. Completing the exchange of notes within twenty-four hours of a meeting will give you the best results.

KEY TAKEAWAYS

- Analyze whether the problem at hand requires a meeting or not.
- Draw a clear objective and create an agenda for your meeting.
- Know your participants and customize the meeting to suit them.
- Don't forget to take notes and mail them to the participants.
- Take care not to digress from the topic using the parking lot concept.
- End the meeting at the designated time or when the objective has been reached.

CHAPTER 22

TELL YOUR STORY

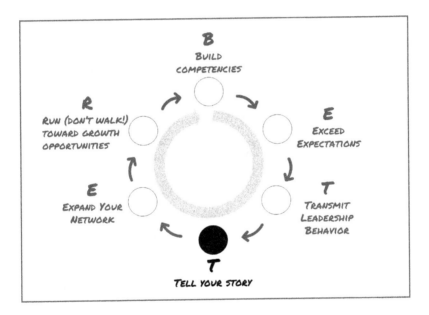

"There is no greater agony than bearing an untold story inside of you."

—Maya Angelou

"Ever read someone's story and think: This is exactly what I needed to hear today! Your story will do that for someone else."

—Anonymous

Opportunities to tell your story happens almost on a daily basis. It could be introducing yourself in a project meeting or just before an important presentation.

DEVELOP A PRESENCE: INTRODUCE YOURSELF CONFIDENTLY

There are opportunities to introduce yourself every day.

Whether you're meeting someone one-on-one, having a team meeting, at a workshop, or at a conference with hundreds of people, there are so many opportunities for you to introduce yourself. Almost half the time, we don't make optimal use of this opportunity.

In a corporate work environment, if you don't brand yourself, other people will brand you. How you introduce yourself defines your personal brand. Having a great introduction is an excellent way of branding, and establishing your presence in a meeting, workshop, or session.

A good introduction will give you instant credibility, as well as spark engagement with other people, and you will come across as a person who knows their stuff.

Reference the Elevator Pitch in the **Moniker Step** in chapter seventeen to really dig deep into this one.

Here's an example as a reminder:

WHO AM I?

My name is Abhijeet.

WHAT BUSINESS AM I IN?

I'm a management consultant who works with high tech companies.

WHOM DO I SERVE?

I advise high tech and software companies around strategy and business operations.

WHAT'S MY SPECIALTY OR USP?

I perform large scale digital transformation around software and the cloud.

WHAT BENEFITS DO CUSTOMERS OR STAKEHOLDERS GET FROM MY WORK?

I help companies realize revenue faster.

Here's how you introduce yourself in a flow:

"Hi, my name is Abhijeet. I'm a management consultant, and I help high tech companies realize revenue faster with digital transformation, especially using SaaS and the cloud."

This introduction takes less than thirty seconds, but it really helps you establish yourself and get your message across.

You can use this entire introduction for everybody, or you can customize it for a specific person or a specific team. But having these five pillars as part of your introduction helps you have a framework around it.

You have to practice delivering your introduction until it becomes second nature to you.

Placing a hook into your introduction, like, "I help companies realize revenues faster" will arouse curiosity in your listeners. Once they're hooked, they may ask, "Oh, that's interesting. How do you do that?" which gives you the chance to advance the conversation.

When you're done with your introduction, always remember to ask the other person, "What do you do?" so that you can connect and engage with them. Having an introduction is probably one of the best opportunities to establish your personal brand in any organization. Hence, regular practice is highly recommended.

When customizing your introduction to a different audience, ask yourself these questions:

- Who is the audience?
- What are they looking for?
- How can you help them?
- How can you create value for the audience?

Answer the above questions with as much detail as possible.

People will always remember how you made them feel. They may not remember every word you said or every presentation you did, but they will surely remember the impact of what you presented. So, make your introduction funny, warm, and welcoming. We often use the phrase "winning the hearts and minds of people." The heart comes before the mind. As you do your introduction, make yourself more collaborative and social, articulate the general value you have, and customize it for that meeting.

PRO TIP

- Customize your story depending on the audience and the environment. You don't want to sound too bombastic for a junior audience or too underwhelming for a senior audience.
- Sharing a story about your personal or professional struggle is often a great way to be vulnerable, establish a strong connection and create an everlasting bond. It's almost as if you are creating a virtual circle of trust by sharing an intense challenge and how you overcame it, or are in the process of addressing.

KEY TAKEAWAYS

- Introduce yourself confidently to command attention.
- In a corporate environment, if you don't brand yourself, someone else will.
- Use your elevator pitch to give a great introduction.

CHAPTER 23

EXPAND YOUR NETWORK

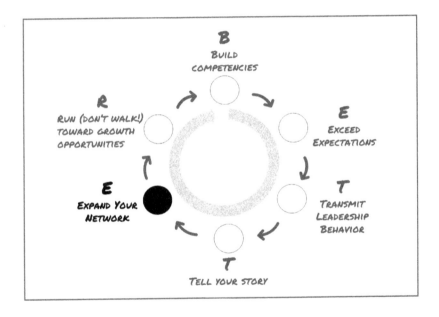

"Your network determines your net worth."

—Anonymous

Your professional network consists of people with whom you have connected throughout your life for career-related or business reasons. The significance of cultivating such a network might not be immediately apparent, especially if you're just starting out in your career which is why you should read this chapter closely. Career experts agree that your network determines your net worth in the career market. While many factors contribute to your early-career opportunities, as you advance in your career, your network becomes the number one driver. Cultivating a vast and valuable network is the best way to find your next opportunity and will turn out to be the most valuable possession you will collect in your life.

The blogosphere is cluttered with startup founders extolling the benefits a professional network has given them. Some even claim to have achieved breakthroughs for their companies solely due to the connections they cultivated.

> Start building your network
> before you need your network.

Don't wait for the need to arise to start building your network. While you're at it, don't hesitate to network with people outside your domain as well. Never miss out on an opportunity to meet new people from diverse backgrounds. For example, you never know when you need a lawyer.

As you build your network, you will realize the growth has a compounding effect. When you add a person to your network, you're also adding yourself to that person's network, which will open you up to a whole new realm of professional networks.

BUT HOW DO YOU BUILD YOUR NETWORK?

The best time to build your network was yesterday. The next best time to build your network is today. As soon as you finish reading this book, formulate an action plan to get going.

Cultivating a great network is energy and time intensive. It is a labor of love that will reap multiple benefits further down your career path when you most need them. The more you put into your network, the more helpful and powerful it can become.

WHO COULD BE IN YOUR NETWORK?

You can have your employers (current and former), customers, friends, and relatives in your network. Just because you left a job doesn't mean you should burn your bridges. You can even have current and past employers of your friends and relatives as well as their customers. Your industry colleagues and peers are also members, as well as people you've met through online social networks like LinkedIn and Facebook. Headhunters and recruiters are a very important part of your network.

Your life-changing opportunity could come through a friend of a friend whom you met on the sidelines of an after-work party.

Your potential for building and scaling your network is massive. If you go closely through the list below, there are a lot of opportunities just waiting to be tapped.

Are all of these people already in your network? Most likely, no. So, it's a great opportunity to go out, network, and bring those people into your LinkedIn or other social platform network as you build it.

NINE WAYS TO BUILD YOUR NETWORK

1. BE HELPFUL

Being helpful is a powerful way to build your network but be genuine when you offer your assistance. What could be a true gift you can give to the other person without being asked? People can always tell if you're being disingenuous despite your best efforts to mask it. When you're offering to help, do so without demanding anything in return. Your genuine drive to help people will leave a lasting impact.

2. BUILD A DIVERSE NETWORK

Go outside your usual social circles and comfort zones. That's where you'll meet new people. Your personality type doesn't matter; just be yourself, and you can build a diverse network. A programmer meets a chef who was catering for a tech-conference and a new food services startup is born. An entrepreneur networks with a lawyer and lays out his difficulties in getting his business off the ground. Just like that, a legal services startup for entrepreneurs is born.

3. BUILD YOUR ONLINE BRAND

Another technique is to really amp up your online game. Every single person that you meet should be connected to your LinkedIn or Facebook profile. Instagram and online forums can be used as networking opportunities. If you're not online, you might as well not exist. Give equal importance to your online brand as you give to your real-world reputation.

4. SOCIAL CAUSES: VOLUNTEER FOR A CHARITY

You can volunteer for a charity where you will meet people who have the same value or perspectives as you do. By meeting people with similar values, you can develop a deeper network.

Remember though, that most people who volunteer do so to get out of their work life and contribute to something meaningful. Their service may be a deeply personal experience for them. Be mindful not to discuss business with them at this time. Instead, take their information and connect with them at a later date.

5. ATTEND CONFERENCES

Attending conferences can help you connect to people who are within your domain or within your professional area. Industry experts are a common sight at conferences. You do not want to miss out on a chance to add them to your network. A confluence of like-minded individuals is also the perfect opportunity to network if you're just starting out on your career.

6. BUILD ONE-ON-ONE CONNECTIONS

Asking for and making an introduction for others is important in building networks. Ask for introductions or make introductions for your friends.

> Your network drives your net worth.

7. ASK FOR REFERRALS

Ask your friends for an introduction to the perfect person in their network they feel you should meet. This is a great way to build a network, especially with people who might be in a very influential role. If your friend is friends with a very influential person, do not shy away from asking for an introduction. This is how some business deals are made.

8. NEVER EAT ALONE

We all have to eat. Why not grab lunch with your colleagues rather than sitting alone and having that sandwich? It is much better to eat with someone and get to know them a little bit better. Food always sparks interesting conversations and sharing a meal is a universal medium for bonding.

9. NURTURE AND KEEP YOUR NETWORK ACTIVE

Figure out how you can help your network (parts of it or individuals). Share information with them that could be relevant. Keep in touch with your network periodically so you're always on their radar.

Start building your network today, and you will never regret it. As compounding happens, your network becomes more and more powerful.

KEY TAKEAWAYS

- Your professional network has the power to catapult your career.
- Always be on the lookout for networking opportunities.
- Curate and cultivate your network.
- Day by day, step by step, slowly build up your network and reap the benefits of compound interest in your career.

CHAPTER 24

RUN (DON'T WALK!) TOWARD GROWTH OPPORTUNITIES

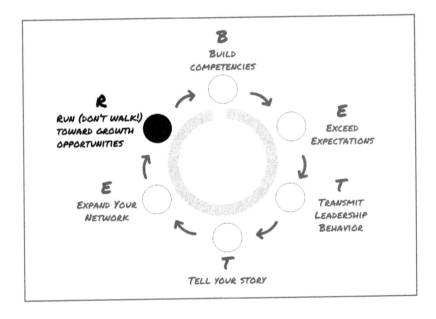

> "Don't wait for the right opportunity: create it."
>
> —George Bernard Shaw

> "If a window of opportunity appears, don't pull down the shade."
>
> —Tom Peters

As you exceed expectations, transmit leadership behavior, and expand your professional network, and you will likely be exposed to growth opportunities. Either those opportunities will present themselves through your network, or you will uncover them on your own.

Not all opportunities will be growth opportunities. A growth opportunity has to have one or more of the following components. The opportunity:

1. Elevates your role to an increasing level of responsibility and accountability.
2. Provides opportunities to learn new skills.
3. Gives you exposure to new domains and new markets.

IDENTIFYING GROWTH OPPORTUNITIES

There are several signs of a potential growth opportunity based on your analysis in the first part of the *Unlock!* 7 Step Process. A potential growth opportunity:

- Is part of one of the trends you identified in Horizon 2 or Horizon 3 in the 3 Horizons Tool in the **Horizon Step** (chapter fifteen) indicating future growth in the area or domain?
- Includes a skill or competency that is in your Learning Plan section in the Career Plan tool of the **North Star** Step (chapter thirteen).
- Places you with a team or organization which is going to experience high growth.
- Is in a highly complex or challenging area which means any improvement you can demonstrate will be recognized and rewarded.

When you see any opportunity that contains any of these components, make sure you run toward it and grab it with both hands. Riding a growth opportunity is intense, exciting, and a great way to accelerate career growth.

When growth opportunities emerge, you have to be prepared for meaningful conversations.

GROWTH OPPORTUNITIES: CONVERSATIONS AND INTERVIEWS

Here is a quick guide to having conversations and interviews internally within your company.

Some of us are super excited by the internal interview process, while others seem to get a bit nervous about it. Let's break down the process and understand how to do interviews effectively. We will go above and beyond the standard interview advice so you can create a game plan to ACE your interviews.

Just for context: in the **Moniker Step** (chapter seventeen), you worked on building your personal brand. You crafted an elevator pitch and put that on your LinkedIn profile. Let's assume you've also created an excellent set of resumes contextualized and customized to the role, the industry, and the organizations you're trying to target. You've also gone through a job search, activated your network, and here you are now, trying to get into an interview.

Now, let's talk about the game plan a little bit. Your game plan is all about making sure that you are set up for the three types of interviews you're going to face.

- **Informational interview,** which is part of your initial conversation with colleagues and executives in the company

- **Video interviews,** these are the actual interview conversations that happen in 1: many or panel settings

SUCCEEDING DURING THE INTERNAL INTERVIEW PROCESS

How do you succeed at the interview process? By knowing what interviewers are looking for.

Great interviewers are always looking for ACE – ability, cultural fit, and eagerness.

- **A is for Ability:** Ability is determined by asking questions like, "Is this person capable? Does this person have the right skill set?"
- **C is for Cultural fit:** This topic can be answered by questions like, "How well will this person fit into our organization? Will she understand and grow our great work culture?" Even within the same company, there are different cultures. Interviewers also often consider the viability of working with the interviewee or spending time with them in the workplace for an extended period. The cultural fit aspect is essential to determine during the hiring process because the new employee is going to be working and interacting with others in the department and possibly a new company location as a team. Bad cultural fit generally leads to unhappy co-workers and less team success.
- **Eagerness: Employers** want to know your levels of hunger and passion – your eagerness. Do you have fuel in the tank to do the job and do it with flair?

Great interviewers are always looking for these three things as they assess candidates. Let's figure out how to put your best foot forward and to showcase your strengths, skills, and experience to ACE these three dimensions.

And then we'll talk a little bit about how to follow up after the interview and how to negotiate and close that offer.

THE INTERVIEW PROCESS

No matter what, the interview process is intense but fulfilling. You not only stand to get a great job because of the interview process, but also gain a lot of knowledge because you're interviewing with so many people. Interviewing also helps you build your network. You can add all the people with whom you interview to your LinkedIn network. To succeed, create a game plan for each interview type.

INFORMATIONAL INTERVIEWS

When you activate your network and have friendly conversations, you begin the informational interview part of the process. These are opportunities to understand what the other person is looking for and to pitch yourself if it's the right fit. Informational interviews may be with hiring managers or someone else within the company.

As we've discussed before, your elevator pitch is a great tool to use to introduce yourself correctly. Follow this up by asking about what's going on in the interviewer's organization, function, area, or projects. Make sure you listen intently and take good notes in your head as these will help you craft your response when it's your turn. Share your ideas and concepts about the target areas. This is a crucial step. All the personal branding exercises you did in the **Moniker Step** – from writing long-form articles to creating blog posts and podcasts – were about sharing your knowledge in this area. At the very least, they will tell the other person that you have a perspective on the industry, even if they don't agree with you.

Toward the end, you can mention that you are looking for a new job. This is an excellent way for you to make sure you've established credibility as well as your brand, before popping the question of wanting to be hired.

Once you've had a great informational interview, you might be asked to participate formally in the interview process. Alternatively, you might have already applied through the company's website or recruiter website or been brought up as a candidate by a current employee within the company, and now you've been asked to participate in the interview process.

ACING THE VIDEO INTERVIEW / DISCUSSION

PS: I know we are talking about video interviews here, but this could apply to any situation where you are having discussions with an organization for a growth role. Capiche?

The game plan for your phone interview is a framework I call ... drumroll ... AMERIKA ☺

It's a set of actions that help you be 100 percent ready for video interviews even they are in a panel situation.

The Amerika Framework will allow you to make sure you're covering all your bases, and you're putting yourself in the best light possible for the phone interview.

A IS FOR ASK

Ask the recruiter for more information prior to the call, like who will interview you. Researching the interviewers is a critical part of a successful process.

M IS FOR MEETING LOGISTICS

Make sure you have the meeting invite, and you understand the logistics. Is there any software to download or is it a simple phone call? Having your earphones for the call is a good idea. Since it's a video call, make sure you are properly dressed and that you have the right background and lighting. I'd recommend an external webcam for high quality video and an external mic for high quality audio. You have to look and sound right for this important conversation.

E IS FOR ENGAGEMENT

Yes, that's right, we will be using the trusted small talk. It is a great way to open a conversion and create engagement. Depending on the interviewer, choose a safe and neutral topic like weather, geography/location, traffic, or stock market. Make sure the topic presents a positive aspect, for example, "What great weather are we having right now," or "The traffic getting into the office was really smooth, no issues." Stay far away from controversial topics like politics.☺

R IS ABOUT THE ROLE

Research the interviewer before the call. Understand the role of this person. Look them up on LinkedIn to figure out how their role is related to the position for which you are interviewing. Identifying the relationship of the job to the role of the interviewer is very important. You will discover whether the interviewer is going to be a direct hiring manager or is someone from another function, a colleague, or a peer. This helps you have a more purposeful interview.

I IS FOR INTEREST

What is this person most interested in knowing? For example, if your interviewer is a finance person, his possible interest areas will be profitability, cost control, etc. If your interviewer is a salesperson, sales metrics might perk his interest. One more quick tip is to figure out the **potential challenges and opportunities** for this person. How do you find out about this? If you know someone in the organization in which you are interviewing, you can ask that person for a little bit of information about the challenges that person faces in that section of the company, or what opportunities are on the horizon. You might also ask about key projects the interviewer may have.

K STANDS FOR KEY MESSAGES

What are going to be your key messages during the phone interview? You should prepare at least three things you can highlight about yourself. Provide any relevant experience that shows you in a good light, anything that shows you that you are a slam dunk for this job.

You can talk about anything that highlights your strengths, such as describing projects similar to ones they are planning or giving examples from the work you've done to drastically change the status quo.

This will put you in the right category of being a fit for the job.

A IS FOR AFFINITY

Affinity is a way for you to establish a connection with the interviewer. You can reference a common geography, a college connection, or mention their favorite brand of coffee. Developing a human connection will show you are someone with whom they can work and that you are a cultural fit.

In addition to the AMERIKA Framework, there are a few things you can do to gain an edge in your interview.

Get knowledge. Call up additional people in the organization with which you are interviewing and ask them about the top projects, internal functions or systems, or anything that can give you an edge.

Carry a notebook to the interview because as your interviewer is introducing or providing information or sharing their responses or perspectives on things, you may want to make some quick notes. Provide a more on-target response by referencing what they've already said.

This extra step shows top partnership and collaboration which is very important in interviews these days.

Prepare a set of questions. Make sure these questions will help you determine whether this is the right job for you. Powerful questions will make sure you are showing yourself in an impressive light, and show you are knowledgeable in the target space. Sometimes asking really good questions is even better than having great answers. This is because the nature of your inquiry shows that you are thinking and have the right mindset to do this job.

Develop a whiteboarding strategy. That brings me to the number one game-changer in your interview. Are you ready for this? Create a whiteboarding strategy for your interview. How do you execute this strategy? Make sure that there is at least a virtual whiteboard during your interview, you can absolutely use the whiteboard features of the video tool with your mouse for this purpose.

Think about three pictures based on your strengths, such as a phenomenal project you delivered or some exceptional business results you have generated. The drawings could be visuals about a technology, a process, or an organizational structure. The only condition is that it must be easy for you to draw them! Using them, you tell a story. Make sure there are enough parts of the story that were challenging so that you show your strengths. Showcase your eagerness and your ability, your grit and determination, and your ability to overcome adversity.

Here's the deal: when you are in the middle of an interview and you see a cue that this could be a good place for you to use one of those three visuals, you should ask for permission to draw a picture for the interviewer. This way, you can take the conversation forward to demonstate your strengths. No interviewer is going to say no. Go to the whiteboard, draw a quick picture, and explain what happened. Provide a story worth telling. Describe what mistakes were made and how things were set right, what challenges there were and how you helped overcome them.

The interviewer will see you as someone ready for the job. The biggest advantage of using this technique is that you are able to tell your story, which no resume can capture. The interviewer's attention moves from the resume to the actual story on the whiteboard, prompting them to ask you more questions because it immediately sparks an interest.

Using the whiteboarding strategy and all the additional advantages it entails, you will be able to ACE the interview. Once again, you show ability, you show you are going to be a great cultural fit, and you show eagerness and passion.

FOLLOW UP

Once you've had a great interview, follow up within twenty-four hours. I recommend doing an email follow-up at the minimum, or if you want to get fancy, you can do it with a letter. Make sure you send a personalized email to each interviewer. If, for some reason, you don't have the interviewer's email, send individual emails to the recruiter and ask the recruiter to forward them to the interviewer.

This establishes a personal connection with the interviewer. After some time, add them to your LinkedIn so that they can see your profile. Maybe they'll notice even additional things about you that will actually seal the deal and get you an offer.

KEY TAKEAWAYS

- Leverage the power of A-ability, C-culture, and E-eagerness to ACE your interviews.
- Follow the AMERIKA Framework to create a game plan that highlights your strengths and gain an edge in the market.
- Adopt the whiteboarding strategy, leaders like leaders who tell stories.

PART F

RENEW

The only constant in life is change.

This fundamental truth presents itself frequently in your career in the form of changes in market trends, company vision, environment, and most of all, in your personal life. The Reinvent part gives you tools to reinvent yourself to take advantage of the changes and trends around you.

This renewal process is crucial in our fast-paced future-oriented careers because we need to rest the engine awhile before we gear up again. Give yourself time and space to regroup and refocus before you continue toward your career goal.

Sometimes, it takes a little distance and deep thinking to assess your progress. What goals have you achieved that you set out to meet in the beginning? Have you been successful in charting your course as a leader? How is your personal brand coming along?

The need to take time off and refocus cannot be overstated. Let me share my tried-and-tested methods with you.

To succeed, you might have to:
a) Reframe the past
b) Reimagine the future AND
c) Reinvent yourself in the present!

SOURCE: WWW.NAPKINSIGHTS.COM/NAPKIN/339/

CHAPTER 25

REINVENT

*"I overcame myself, the sufferer; I carried my own ashes
to the mountains; I invented a brighter flame for myself."*

— Friedrich Nietzsche, *Thus Spoke Zarathustra*

*"Your power to choose your direction of your life allows you to reinvent yourself,
to change your future, and to powerfully influence the rest of creation."*

—Stephen Covey

I have a simple rule to change things in my work life. When I
observe that I am no longer learning anything new, I make
changes.

This simple rule has survived the test of time for me and many of the
amazing professionals I have coached. Abiding by it makes sure we
refresh ourselves and keep upgrading our skills and knowledge.

When should we think about the rule? How often?

The ability to reinvent is critical, actually mandatory, for your
healthy and long career.

It puts you in a mental space where you can:

- Review how you have been doing, professionally speaking
- Define what market opportunities lie ahead
- Determine what can you do to take advantage of those opportunities and create value
- Decide if you need to make a major or minor career pivot

If you are thinking this sounds a bit like what we've already covered earlier in *Unlock!*, you are absolutely right. We are going to reference the work that you have already done from steps one through six. But there is a major difference: in the **Reinvent Step**, you are putting yourself in a mental space where you are intentionally looking to make a pivot.

Enter one of my favorite career hacks: a personal offsite retreat. A personal offsite retreat is an event where you take the time out of your regular schedule and go to a different physical location for reflection, self-care, and planning ahead.

Yep! I like to do this on a quarterly basis. Every three to four months, you will find me wandering off into the woods in Northern California or huddled up in a café in San Francisco. I like to spend the entire day with myself to reflect and plan.

GETTING READY FOR REINVENT: PERSONAL PERFORMANCE TRACKER

Most of us have hectic workdays, and we tend to forget accomplishments that have happened over such a significant period of time. The best and the only solution here is to create your own performance tracker, which is a reasonably easy process. Let us see how it works.

Use the Performance Tracker spreadsheet from the download section.[18]

PERFORMANCE TRACKER TOOL

#	Date	Project	Quick Description	Sponsor / Stakeholder	Value	Feedback	Metrics
	Date of the project or event	Title of the project	What was this project or work effort about?	Who were the sponsors / key executives / stakeholders for the project?	What specific value did you create for this project?	Did you get any written or verbal feedback? Be sure to store a copy of email that you've received	Capture any metrics that quantify the value you created; this might be hard in some cases
1							
2							
3							
4							

The intent of the tracker is to capture key pieces of information related to your performance. These typically include:

- Feedback you have received via email, text, or in person
- Words of encouragement or kudos received
- Specific areas, teams, and people whom you have helped: these might be one-off situations or help that you provided over a period of time

The following pieces of information are **important**:

1. **Date:** The date of this event

2. **Project or Initiative:** Title of the project you are working on

3. **Sponsor:** Who is the sponsor, executive, or steering committee for that project?

4. **Value:** What is the value or enhancement you provided for this project? What was your role? How did you make the change happen?

---

18 Download all templates and bonus material at www.unlockthebook.com/resources

5. **Feedback:** What feedback did you get from the sponsor or from the team? Can you mention the feedback here? Do you have an email that you can attach? Alternatively, print a copy or download it to your computer.

6. **Metrics:** Capture any metrics that were shared that quantify the impact that you had.

Every couple of weeks or so, record these events and achievements in your Personal Performance Tracker.

1. Write down the details of the project, the project objective, and what it was supposed to solve.

2. Write down the name of the stakeholder (it can be a team, a person, or an executive) and the outcome that was created. Ask yourself questions like, "Did you do an excellent presentation?" "Did you help another team with a customer?" Those questions help you analyze your performance. The outcome is anything positive.

3. And most importantly, ask the stakeholder you helped to email your manager. This allows you to have a written document regarding the task and informs your manager you have accomplished an outcome and done a great job.

If you do this tracking regularly, you will have a comprehensive library of tasks and achievements. It not only contains the work you did, but it also includes specifics of the emails and communication from all the people that you've supported. This creates data points that genuinely help with your performance review.

Building your own performance tracker can be a great help in your professional life. It's a great way to prepare for the next activity in the **Reinvent Step**: your Personal Offsite Retreat.

Pro tip: In the Personal Performance Tracker, you are documenting every single one of your achievements, which includes the things that would have gone unnoticed, for which you may end up getting a raise. In some cases, it might save your job as well!

PERSONAL OFFSITE RETREAT: REFLECTION POOL

Choose a location for your retreat that is in contrast to your usual work location and home location. A location that breaks your usual pattern and creates a "pattern interrupt," a hack that refreshes the mind and gets you into a growth thinking mindset pretty quickly.

Pro tip: Make sure to have completed the Personal Performance Tracker tool before heading out to your Personal Offsite Retreat.

Here's an outline of how I run my own Personal Offsite Retreat that you can use.

I take the time to reflect on what has happened since the last time I took time off to reflect and plan. The Personal Performance Tracker tool comes in very handy for this step.

1. **Reflection**: What has happened? What has been my progress? Did I add value to my organization, my team? Did I add value to my family, friends and community? What is that value? Can I measure it?

2. **Acknowledgement**: What have been my accomplishments and failures? Could I have done some things differently?

3. **Gratitude**: Who are the people that have been helping me? How can I express gratitude and thank them?

4. **Evaluate**: What should I do next? What changes should I make? What opportunities lie ahead that I can take advantage of? What value can I add? Should I be making any small or large

career moves? Which skills should I learn? How should I enhance my network? Here, you can reference the tools you have been using from steps one through six.

Take time to disconnect from everything and focus on reflection. Half a day is minimum prescription dosage, but you can take the entire day for this exercise. The **Reinvent Step** can help you plan for the time.

Look at macro and micro trends: During this time, you are not only evaluating your progress but also looking at the macro and micro trends around you.

Reflect on needed adjustments long-term plans: Evaluate your career progress against your long-term goals and determine what adjustments you need to make to stay on track and achieve them as planned.

Pro tip: You can go back and update your Career Plan that we developed in the **North Star** Step (chapter thirteen) so that you can keep it current and work on the new items.

Meet your coach or mentor(s): Set up a time to meet your mentors and coaches to think and talk through career progress and any upcoming transitions. You can then work with your coach to figure out how to continue to make progress as well as take bigger leaps into bigger opportunities for your career.

KEY TAKEAWAYS

- It is important to have a personal offsite to reinvent and plan ahead.
- A clean performance review not only helps you get a raise but also might save your job.
- Write down your weekly achievements in the Personal Performance Tracker to keep track of them.

RESOURCES

- Personal Performance Tracker

All tools mentioned in the book can be downloaded from www.unlockthebook.com/resources

PART G

PUTTING IT ALL TOGETHER

You spend most of your waking time either at work or thinking about work. With all the tools that you learned in the Unlock! journey, it is time to put them in action.

Remember, the universe always rewards actions, not ideas or plans.

In this section, you will see how we can put Unlock! tools into action and how you can make investments in your career.

Similar to a financial portfolio, you can make investments in your career to create compounded growth for yourself: daily, weekly, monthly and annually.

1. 2.

AWESOME

FOR YOU TO CREATE A "LABOR OF LOVE", THAT THE WORLD CALLS "AWESOME", YOU GOT TO LOVE THE LABOR FIRST!

SOURCE: WWW.NAPKINSIGHTS.COM/NAPKIN/805/

CHAPTER 26

TAKE ACTION

"The secret of getting ahead is getting started."

—Mark Twain

The *Unlock!* 7 Step Process is all about action. This methodology unlocks your potential career opportunities and unleashes the leader inside you. The **North Star, Discovery, Horizon,** and **Resolve Steps** and their accompanying tools point out the ways to define your career direction and unlock career opportunities once invisible to you. The **Moniker Step** guides you to develop your branding and promote visibility as a leader in your particular domain. The **Elevate Step**'s Leadership Flywheel helps you take your performance as a leader to the next level and accelerate your career growth.

Now, let's put it together along with a heady mix of free market capitalism and the Dalai Lama.

Ready? Let's go.

INVESTING WISELY

Investing in your career is very similar to making financial investments. Over a period of time, these investments are going to give you returns. One of the most intriguing things about your career is optimally applying what you learn gives you a higher rate of return than even some of the financial investments you make.

One of the other areas where career investments are similar to financial investments is the area of compound interest. Investments yield a higher return through compounding. The investments you make in your career not only give you quick wins in the short term but give you massive wins over a longer period of time. As we have seen the chapters on the Elevate Leadership Flywheel, spinning the flywheel creates compounding returns.

Your career is going to need investments and those investments are going to come in the form of not just time but also money. Now let's look at some of the areas where you can invest in to get great returns.

Learning: You know that learning is your number one career superpower. From a goals standpoint, make sure you are including learning goals in the Learning Plan section of the Career Plan of **North Star Step.**

> Your network drives your net worth.

Networking: Initially, when you're new in your career, your education and experience will get you new opportunities. But as you progress in your career over a period of time, it's your network that really propels you and provides you the basis for even more career opportunities.

Mentors and coaches: As you might have seen in the Elevate Leadership Flywheel, having mentors is extremely valuable. I highly recommend having not just mentors, but also having a coach. A lot of times we are so caught up in our own world that we may be oblivious to the opportunities around us. A coach shines a light on these opportunities.

Tech: Identify the types of apps and devices that can help you be more productive. Using them ensures you can invest more in your career with the limited resources you might have. Here are my favorite applications that you might want to invest in:

1. **LinkedIn Premium:** The premium version enables you to make deeper searches, view profiles, and send InMail. It also includes LinkedIn Learning, which makes it a great tool.

2. **Social media tools:** Facebook, Instagram, and Twitter go a long way in keeping your network active.

3. **A great laptop:** Productivity is a great lever for our careers. You owe it to your career to invest in a high-performance machine like a MacBook Pro or a Surface Pro. For me, just the ability to open up the laptop and start typing is worth the ticket price. The increase in productivity justifies the incremental cost of a high-end computer.

4. **Smartphone and apps:** Get the best smartphone possible and get apps that can help you with productivity, time arbitrage, or learning. Here are some app investments that are worth it:

   a. **MENTAL HEALTH**
      i. **Calm and Mindspace:** Make time to meditate. Find your center. Improve mental and spiritual health.
   b. **WORK FROM ANYWHERE / PRODUCTIVITY**

i Slack: Productivity for teams.

ii OneNote or Evernote: Phenomenal note taking that syncs across devices. Sweet.

iii. Zoom / WebEx / Hangouts: Video calling and meetings.

iv. Food delivery apps: Though I prefer homemade food, this is a great help when it's crunch time.

v. Booster Fuel: Get gas while you are away or at work. No more detours and stopping at gas stations.

c. PROFESSIONAL NETWORKING

i. LinkedIn Premium: Expand your professional network and keep it active.

ii. Blind: Get the scoop on internal company matters. Listen from people in other companies. Great career insider information.

d. LEARNING

i Kindle: For reading and learning.

ii. Coursera and Udemy: Affordable training resources.

iii. Apple Podcasts or Spotify: Keep learning while you are walking the dog. Or just walking. Or running.

iv. YouTube: For learning. I know, it is easy to while away time on this one. But it is a great resource for learning almost anything.

v. Overdrive and Libby: Download books and audiobooks from your local library. For FREE!

e. WHEN WE ARE BACK TO NORMAL ☺

i. SpotHero: Find and book parking spots in busy cities. This helps you save time.

ii. Uber or Lyft: These apps offer better commute options. Time arbitrage galore.

     iii. **Waze:** Save time by avoiding busy routes. Plus, it has cop alerts.

  f. **PERSONAL FINANCE APPS**

     i. Personal Capital

     ii. Credit Karma

Mental, physical, and spiritual health: The Dalai Lama once said, "Man sacrifices his health to make money. Then he sacrifices money to recuperate his health." Your good health is the basis of having a really successful career, because a great career will not matter if you have bad health. It is important to note that having mental and spiritual health is as important as maintaining physical health.

HOW TO MAKE CAREER INVESTMENTS

Now that we know where to make career investments, let's look at how we can make those investments. My recommendation is to use a calendar-based approach for investing in your career. It's similar to a financial investment approach which most of you might know as dollar-cost averaging. In this approach, we make investments over a period of time, making time the mechanism to trigger those investments.

Let's review our calendars on a daily, weekly, monthly, and quarterly basis to make career investments.

MAKING DAILY INVESTMENTS

1. Learning

Learning is a superpower that you should exercise and amp up. Learning happens in different forms and everyone has a primary learning style. Develop self-evaluation and self-awareness to understand your ideal way to learn. While some people learn better through audio and video, others learn better through kinesthetics, which is learning by doing. For example, I like to subscribe to podcasts and videos which will help me learn even when walking, running, or doing chores.

2. Apply learning

Learn something new about a particular topic in a different and more meaningful way. Once you learn it, you can start putting it into practice the same day.

3. Mental, physical, and spiritual health

Figuring out a span of time for your mental, physical and spiritual health is important. That's how you start to invest on a daily basis in your health.

MAKING WEEKLY INVESTMENTS

Plan to make weekly investments in your career. This begins with having a clear plan for the week.

Manage your calendar on a weekly basis: At the beginning of every week, go over your schedule. Work with the visibility you have at hand.

Allocating time to your highest priority: During this planning, you must allocate blocks of time to the complete highest priority at work first.

Block time: Once you've blocked time for the highest work priority, block time for yourself because you need to get some other work done, including time for personal growth. You have many responsibilities. You need to make plans, build those skills, and make sure you are learning, as well as contributing to your company and your team.

Schedule networking meetings: This is how you build your network. As you look at your weekly calendars over a period of time, think about the people whom you want to meet on a regular basis or on an irregular basis. Make sure you schedule those meetings ahead of time. This allows you to keep your network alive and grow it.

MAKING MONTHLY INVESTMENTS

This is the time to reflect on the accomplishments and challenges of the previous month, as well as plan the upcoming month.

Review prior month: Review the previous month. Evaluate and decide whether you are making the supposed progress or not. Determine what adjustments must be made if you are not on track for where you want, or must, be.

Review progress against personal and professional goals: A career plan that has goals written down is the real plan. Everything else that we all think we should be doing is just a pipe dream. It is so important that you write down a set of goals and a career plan.

Review your Career Planning Tool developed during the **North Star** Step of the *Unlock!* 7 Step Process (chapter thirteen). Check your progress toward your goals to be sure you are learning the necessary things for your goal.

Sign up for conferences and trainings: Look at future conferences/training available in your industry, both in-person and virtual. Which ones do you need to register for this month? What do you need to do to get your company to pay for the training? If they won't pay, you'll need to invest your own time and money into these events to learn more and grow your network.

MAKING QUARTERLY INVESTMENTS

This is the time to take a more intense look at your career progress.

Running your own Personal Offsite Retreat: Take time to disconnect from everything and focus on reflection. Half a day is minimum prescription dosage, but you can take the entire day for this exercise. The **Reinvent Step** (chapter twenty-four) can help you plan for the time.

Look at macro and micro trends: During this time, you are not only evaluating your progress but also looking at the macro and micro trends around you.

Reflect on needed adjustments to achieve long-term plans: Evaluate your career progress against your long-term goals and determine what adjustments you need to make to achieve them.

Meet your coach or mentor(s): Set up a time to meet your mentors and coaches to think and talk through career progress and any upcoming transitions. You can then work with your coach to figure out how to continue to make progress as well as take bigger leaps into bigger opportunities for your career.

TURN YOUR PLAN INTO REALITY, EASILY

> *"80 percent of success is just showing up."*
>
> —Woody Allen

Here's the hack that will make this real for you: you can take advantage of your calendar software on your computer and schedule all of these things in advance! All the work blocks, meetings, conferences, offsite retreats that you need to have – just put them on the calendar in advance.

Adding everything to the calendar makes you commit to this

schedule and also defines allowable meeting times for others. Automagically, you will see those investments made in your career propel you to becoming a successful leader.

YOUR TWO TRUE FRIENDS IN THIS JOURNEY

Your true friends in this journey toward becoming a successful leader are **effort** and **patience.**

You will have some small and quick wins as you're investing in your career using this approach. But massive wins are going to come over a period of time. Patience is a virtue which will take you much farther.

This investment strategy gives you big breakthroughs over a period of time. Make sure to invest in those things regularly – daily, monthly, weekly, and quarterly – and make even more progress.

Putting in effort and hustling is absolutely required day to day. From a big picture standpoint, you have to be patient. The market will reward you sooner or later. That is a given. Effort in the micro and patience in the macro wins the game for you.

EXPONENTIAL GROWTH

The Elevate Leadership Flywheel creates massive results due to compounding. Each step of the wheel automatically leads to the next step. The first few steps of moving the flywheel will feel difficult. It is natural. But as you keep pushing, it will start to build momentum. From then on, the flywheel keeps on turning and creating results for you.

The *Unlock!* 7 Step Process contains a flywheel to achieve tremendous career results. It won't be an easy task, and it will obviously be hard. But as you start performing activities based on the flywheel regularly, you will eventually gain momentum. That is when new opportunities start knocking on your door.

As I've coached individuals and teams, I've observed changes in months, weeks, and in some cases, days.

But if you feel that these changes are not happening fast enough, dig deeper and reflect to see what you need to enhance or tweak your strategy and plan. Sometimes a breakthrough is a matter of fine-tuning certain approaches and communication styles.

Or you might be a Chinese bamboo tree.

The Chinese bamboo tree is no less than any other tree. It also requires nurturing like any other plant. But you won't witness any signs of activity in its first year. There won't be any growth above the soil in the following years either. You might feel as if your patience is being tested. But yet you keep watering the area and nurturing it. Just as you might start losing hope ... voila! The tree shoots up more than eighty feet in just six weeks.

The result is amazing, but it is the culmination of years of hard work, nurturing, effort ... and patience.

LEADERSHIP IS ACTION: YOUR JOURNEY TO BECOME A SUCCESSFUL LEADER

Leadership is action. It is the culmination point of your thoughts, strategies, learnings, and insights into an act or action.

This book is about taking action to unlock the leader within you and demonstrate leadership actions that create value for others.

Transform your career from just "doing your job" to a continuum of leadership actions.

The **North Star** Step helps you imagine and plan a career that you want and manifest leadership actions. Performing the activities from the **Elevate Step** starts to turn the Elevate Leadership Flywheel. In this flywheel, each step automatically leads to the next.

The flywheel creates compound returns.

It feels hard to turn the flywheel. But you have to keep pushing. It will start to build momentum.

The flywheel effect compounds the return. As Jim Collins says, "You're pushing no harder than during the first rotation, but the flywheel goes faster and faster. Each turn of the flywheel builds upon work done earlier, compounding your investment of effort[19]."

The flywheel will generate results that are far beyond your current plan.

As the **North Star** Step and Elevate Leadership Flywheel take effect, you become aware of the transformation that's happening within you. As the transformation starts to take hold, it becomes visible externally.

You might have observed what happens to potted plants in your living room. As the plant grows, it gets to a size which becomes larger than the pot it is in. At that point, you realize that you need to put the plant in a larger pot because it has outgrown its current pot.

As you take action and demonstrate leadership, you will outgrow your role. You will find yourself moving to bigger roles. All you did was put the strategy and flywheel in action.

The universe of business works in many interesting ways. The ultimate truth is that this universe rewards actions. It may value

---

19 Collins, Jim, *Good to Great: Why Some Companies Make the Leap and Others Don't*, (Harper-Collins, 2001, ISBN: 978-0066620992)

thoughts and ideas, but action is the only way to manifest them and turn them into reality.

That is why taking action with the *Unlock!* 7 Step Process helps you become a successful leader. Automagically.

Here is looking to a new you. Version 2.0.

ACKNOWLEDGEMENTS

I was not planning to write a book. Or this book. Ever. Never ever. Thank you to my mentors and co-conspirators, I was voluntold (yes, that is a technical word) to write this book.

Thank you dear **Rajesh Setty** for believing in me and my abilities to bring a book to this world. Thank you to **Arun Nithyanandam**, you are a treasure trove of brilliant ideas and I managed to steal some from you.

Thank you to the entire team at Verbinden Communication who make my work so much easier: **Girish KN, Vinay Kumar, Arun Kurian Philip, Thomas C Thomas, Sujatha Reghunathan, Likith Kumar, Veeresha Hogesoppinavar and Vivek Rao Vijendra.**

Special gratitude to **Casey Dawes** for making sure my stream of consciousness becomes content that is a joy to read.

Thank you to my publishers: **Rohit Bhargava** and the team at **Vicara Books** for their amazing support and guidance to get the book in the hands of readers.

Thank you **Pamela Slim**, who has been my mentor and an amazing role model for so many years, for writing the foreword for this book. Keep rocking, Pam!

Thank you to my industry peers, former colleagues and managers who believed in me and wrote advance praise for the book: **Aashish Chandorkar, Alejandro Danylszyn, Brian Lillie, Danis Yadegar, Joe Pinto, Johanna Lyman, Jonathan Copulsky, Kaushik Bhaumik, Rajesh Setty, and Tom Berghoff.**

Special thanks to **Rajesh Setty** for his Napkinsights, which are sprinkled throughout this book and tell us some simple truths.

Thank you, Joshua Rozario and his team at Mindshare Digital for their marketing genius.

Thank you, Jill Beaverson for your amazing PR support.

Thank you, Enosh Wilson for the amazing book cover art.

Thank you to my friends who I put through a lot; they had to read early versions of the book: **Abhijit Thosar, Anurag Gupta, Aditya Deshmukh, Bhushan Shinkre, Milind Gurjar, Naval Gupta**, and so many others.

Finally: I'm so thankful to my family who have supported me through thick and thin. My **Aai** and **Baba** have given me the most amazing foundation and love any kid would hope for ... and thank you for not giving up on me. Thank you to **Amol, Kanchan, Anouska** for always being there for me and being my pillars of support. Thank you **Sahasrabudhe Aai, Baba, Prasad, Dinika, Reya**, and **Riaan**; I so appreciate your love and support.

Finally, thank you **Anish** and **Rohan**: you guys are the love of my life, and I learn something from you every day. **Radhika**: you are the real reason for everything I do, and you are the kind of leader whom I aspire to be; thank you for being my best friend and for sharing your life with me.

Thank you to all the challenges and difficulties that appeared at various times in my life that guided me to become who I am today.

With great love, respect and gratitude,

Abhijeet

BIBLIOGRAPHY

- Adams, Scott. *How to Fail at Almost Everything and Still Win Big: Kind of the Story of My Life:* Portfolio, 2014.
- Andreesen, Marc. *Why Software is Eating the World:* Wall Street Journal, 2011.
- Canfield, Jack. *The Success Principles: How to Get from Where You Are to Where You Want to Be:* William Morrow Paperbacks, 2006.
- Coley, Steve. *Enduring Ideas: The Three Horizons of Growth:* McKinsey Quarterly, 2009.
- Collins, Jim. *Good to Great: Why Some Companies Make the Leap and Others Don't:* Harper Collins, 2001.
- Collins, Jim and Porras, Jerry I. *Built to Last:* Successful Habits of Visionary Companies: HarperCollins Publishers, 2011.
- Cuddy, Amy and Caroline A. Wilmuth, Andy J. Yap, Dana Carney. *Preparatory Power Posing Affects Nonverbal Presence and Job Interview Performance:* Journal of Applied Psychology, 2015.
- Dweck, Carol. *The Power of Believing You Can Improve:* Ted Talks, 2014.
- Gallo, Carmine. *The Art of the Elevator Pitch:* Harvard Business Review, 2018.
- *Gartner Forecasts Worldwide Public Cloud Revenue to Grow 17.5 Percent in 2019:* Gartner Press Release, 2019.
- Harter, Jim. *Employee Engagement on the Rise in the US:* Gallup, 2018.
- Minto, Barbara. *The Minto Pyramid Principle: Logic in Writing and Thinking:* Minto International, 1987.
- Myers, Blanka. *Women and Minorities in Tech, By the Numbers:* Wired, 2018.
- Pressfield, Steven. *The War of Art: Break Through the Blocks and Win Your Inner Creative Battles:* Black Irish Entertainment, 2012.
- Sharma, Robin. *The Leader Who Had No Title: A Modern Fable on Real Success in Business and in Life:* Free Press, 2010.
- Slim, Pamela. *Body of Works: Finding the Thread That Ties Your Story Together:* Portfolio, 2013.